Four Legendary Women from Ancient China

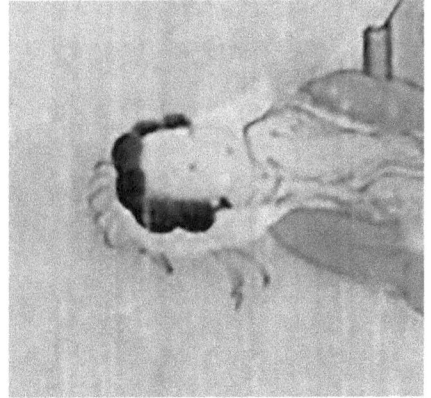

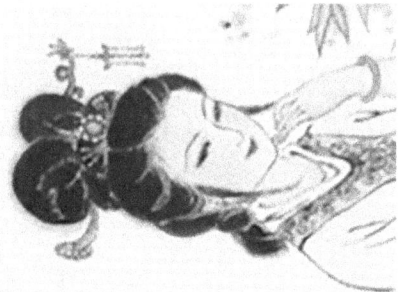

Narrated
by Feng Ping

Published in Australia by

Heart Space Publications
PO Box 1190
Bakery Hill, Victoria, 3354, Australia
Tel +61 450260348

www.heartspacepublications.com
pat@heartspacepublications.com

Whilst every care has been taken to check the accuracy of the
information in this book, the publisher cannot be held responsible
for any errors, omissions or originality.

_Copyright: Text by Feng Ping
Published in Melbourne, Australia in April 2021

ISBN: 978-0-6489215-3-0

Contents

About the author

Feng Ping was born in Shanxi province, China. She gained her Ph.D. at the University of Warsaw, where she studied International Relations with a focus on China's foreign policy towards Central Eastern European countries.

She plays chess, enjoys classical music, and reads widely.

This is her third book. Her first published work was Roads Seeking and her second was Love in Warsaw. She wrote these in Poland during her studies there.

Introduction

Stories of talented ladies and gifted scholars are popular all over the world. Chinese history is full of legendary females, even though in ancient China moral codes were more severely imposed on women. It was extremely hard for a woman to succeed; in fact, it was almost impossible. But there were exceptions. I happened to read an ancient Chinese novel, *Flowers in the Mirror*, which discusses talented and famous Chinese ladies who pursued their career in ancient China. The book inspired me to discover the stories of famous ladies throughout Chinese history. I wanted to show a different aesthetic appreciation of Chinese women of the past. I was amazed at what I found. By researching and documenting the facts of their stories, I believe people from all over the world will be able to enjoy them.

These stories are based on real people, but I have taken the liberty of giving greater personality to the characters than the history books offer.

At the end of each story is a bibliography for that lady and the time during which she lived.

Preface

In the long history of Chinese civilisation, there are many legendary ladies who showed great talent in literature, music, and art, and demonstrated excellent political skill. Some of these women even managed to break the chains of the feudal codes, often for the sake of love. Others determined their own values by making determined choices. Some were able to rise through the ranks of officialdom, that was, until their beauty faded or misfortune plagued them. Because of the exciting time these people lived in, their names were carved in the rock of history. The four legendary women in this book experienced the vicissitudes of life. They were passionate in love, talented in literature, and deeply attached to their homeland. All these years later, their stories are still told, immortalised in the hearts of the Chinese people.

The four women we will discover throughout this book are:

Cai Wenji,	a musical genius;
Shangguan Wan'er,	the first female prime minister of the Tang dynasty;
Zhuo Wenjun,	who conducted three risky chess moves throughout her life;
and Li Qingzhao,	the first female poet in a thousand years.

It was due to their loving and giving natures that they are seen as bright flowers, both for their beauty and charms, as well as their wisdom and sagely advice.

The river of history continues to flow. Sometimes, I wonder whether history created them, or they created history.

Story One

The Musical
Genius of
Cai Wenji

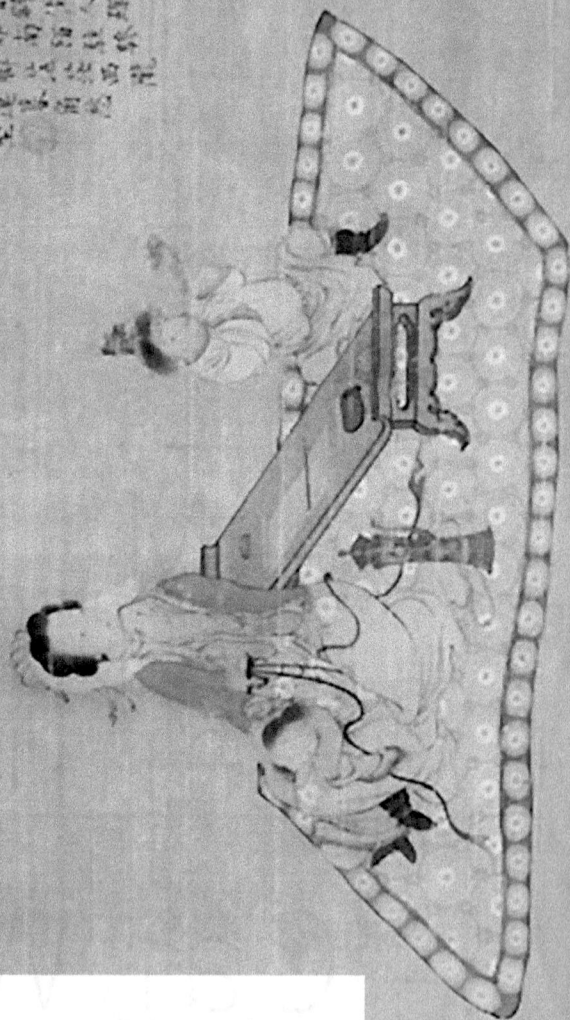

Cai Wenji missed Han.

Painted in Qing dynasty by a famous painter, Li Jian. It reflects Cai Wenji, married to Hun, and missing her Han homeland and people.

Chapter One

Childhood

Cai Wenji was born into a large scholarly gentry family during the Han dynasty (202 BC – 220 AD). The Gods always makes light of a person's fate, as if Cai Wenji was born in peaceful times, with her genius and beauty, she would have been ensured world fame. Unfortunately, this extraordinary woman was born during the troubled times at the end of Eastern Han dynasty (25 BC–220 AD). It was a time when loyal officials were murdered, and when heroes and warlords fought to take or defend their territory; where bandits flourished, robberies and murders were commonplace, and the people starved and were destitute.

However, Cai Wenji had a peaceful and pleasant childhood, as being born into the elite class she was immune to the troubles. Greatly influenced by her father, she read avidly on many topics, and began composing verse, odes, and songs from a very young age.

Her father, Cai Han, was a well-known scholar, erudite in astronomy, politics and calligraphy.

Cai Han was a tall man, with a strong jaw that revealed his candid character. His voice was magnetic and attracted listeners; he was also very persuasive and offered many opinions on a range of topics. He was not only respected by the hierarchy, but also by the common people. Every day, Cai Han's courtyard was like a fair, full of guests who came to talk about politics, music, and literature.

Cai Han enveloped himself in scholarly writings and dedicated his time to dealing with the state affairs of the Han dynasty. However, he could not stop the trend of history as the dynasty sunk further into decline. His remonstrations of the emperor were to no avail. Sometimes, he could not help sighing as he was farsighted enough to see the approaching conflict between the warlords. The region was no longer safe. It would be divided by continuous warfare. Already, the common people were living in hunger and want. One time, he looked up at the sky, and saw a meteorite flashing, leaving a moment of brightness behind, he could not help sighing, thinking to himself: *What an amazing sky it is! However, all its glory is consumed in a flash. I must leave something of profound and long-lasting importance before the dynasty is ruined! I will endeavour to write our history honestly. People should be able to learn where they came from and who they are.*

Cai Han's marriage was childless until he reached the age of forty-five. One day, when Cai Han came back from the court after attending a frustrating day with the emperor, he rushed directly to his wife Zhao Wuniang's chamber with a mix of concern and excitement. He put behind him the travails of the court. He did not want his wife to worry about him, as this was the very day that Zhao Wuniang gave birth to their child, Cai Wenji.

The moment he stepped into house, he asked the servant with apprehension "What's happening, what's happening?"

I am going to be a father! Cai Han burst out laughing. Never had he felt such joy. *Would it be a boy or girl?* Cai Han could not stop his thoughts from racing. What difference – boy or a girl? If a boy, he would educate his son to be a famous scholar. If a girl... he would allow her to receive the same education... if she wanted. Again, he chuckled to himself for being so sentimental. *What a silly old man I am!*

Despite the troubles of the times, I will try my utmost to give the child the best home and safety, no matter the dynasty's situation!

Cai Han walked pass the screen, and went to the bed, which was at the wall opposite the door. A curtain hung before the bed; a table next to it. Cai Han saw Zhao Wuniang had had a difficult birth.

"It is a girl!" announced the servant, who took the baby to Cai Han, who then carefully held her in his arms. His heart burst with joy as he studied this tiny baby, who seemingly watched him as her little arms waved innocently with a static movement.

"What a beautiful child!" Cai Han said with an ear-to-ear smile. Yes, indeed, the baby's large wondering eyes now stared at this big smiling man in front of her and the strange world around her. *How innocent she is – a piece of blank paper. But how was she going to colour the paper of her life in the future? Who will this tiny girl become*?

Zhao Wuniang said with a tired smile, "Sorry, it's not a boy."

"Never mind that, take it easy. Girls and boys are the same to me." Cai Han said as he kissed his wife tenderly on her forehead.

习习习习习

They named the girl Cai Yan. 'Yan' means 'beautiful jade' in Chinese. Cai Han hoped that his daughter would radiate and shine like the best jade. Cai Yan's nickname was Cai Wenji. So, the father addressed his daughter as Wenji.

Born into a privileged household, and to an elderly father, Wenji was greatly indulged. As she grew, he allowed her to read as many books as she wanted and even taught her classical writing.

Wenji showed extraordinary talent from the very beginning. She had long black hair, which reached her waist. Her lovely face was always smiling, as she cared nothing about worldly troubles. As all children should, she grew up carefree. She had a lively and vivacious character, and liked to debate with her father about politics, literature, and books.

Soon, the books her father gave her to read were no longer enough for Wenji. She secretly read all the volumes on her father's bookshelf. Love books were forbidden to her, but she found every opportunity she could to read them in secret. One day she found a book titled *How to Be a Good Woman,* written by a female historian named Ban Zhao in the early Eastern Han dynasty. This book aroused Wenji's interest.

It read, "..... *As a woman, I have been married to Cao's family since I was fourteen years old. Besides helping my brother write history, I worked hard day and night doing housework in Cao's family – afraid that the family would drive me away if I was lazy. In my marriage, what worried me most was the fear that my children would not become useful men in society. As a woman, I try to share my concerns with women who have the same doubts and worries. Not being so busy these days, I dared to write these seven chapters of moral ethnics describing how to be a good woman. I hope my humble effort inspires later generations.*

Firstly, as a woman, it is good to be humble and soft in character. A woman's duty is to take care of the family, which is both simple and yet complicated. A good woman must be diligent in carrying out housework.

Secondly, a good woman needs to marry when she reaches a proper age. After marriage, she needs to treat her husband wholeheartedly with respect.

Thirdly, good women should be prudent in behaviour. Men are stronger than women, both physically and mentally, so in a good household, men should be as strong as high mountains, while women should be as soft as water. Women do not have any advantage in strength, but we could avoid making mistakes by behaving prudently.

Fourthly, a woman should be virtuous. To be a good woman, we must process four qualities in our character: maintain good virtue, be prudent in speaking, look after one's appearance, and develop one's talents. Among them, being virtuous is one of the most important qualities for being a good woman.

Finally, we should be loyal and faithful to our husband. According to The Book of Rites *(a book on ritual and behaviour) men have the right to marry a second wife, but women should never marry a second husband...*

Wenji hungrily read Ban Zhao's book, but at the end she was confused. A rebellious thought crept into her mind, *who is this woman who dared to write such doctrines? What right did she have to preach to women with these stupid ideals... and to plant moral ethical codes in innocent ladies' hearts!* Wenji felt a spasm in her stomach. She dropped the book on the floor, afraid to touch it, as if a flame would scorch her fingers. It was at this moment that her father came in. He could see her confusion and agitation. Her father could not help feeling alarmed and asked, "What's wrong, my dear?"

Wenji said nothing but pointed to the book on the floor. Cai Han saw the title, *How to Be a Good Woman*, and immediately understood his daughter's confusion and troubled mind.

He picked up the book and asked, "Do you have any questions that are bothering you?"

With pursed her lips and in an unhappy tone she asked, "Who is the author of this book?" Her hands were trembling. She knew that this book showed the subservient future that she was likely to face.

"She was a great female writer, a historian and a scholar in early times. Much the same as you, she was born into an intellectual family, where she was not required to do any sewing or housework. She spent most of her time studying books."

"Oh!" Cai Wenji immediately changed her attitude towards Ban Zhao, although she was still confused.

"Bao Zhao was a legend, very brilliant. Her brother was Ban Gu, who was given the task by the emperor to write the history of the Han dynasty. However, he didn't finish it before he died, so Ban Zhao continued his work. Thereafter, she became famous for her prose. One of the most famous works that she wrote was this book."

"Why did she emphasise her marriage to Cao's family?" Cai Wenji asked with concern.

"It was because the Cao family was one of the most important in the Eastern Han dynasty. That's why she wrote *How to Be a Good Woman*. She wrote as a privileged woman from a well-to-do family. It was understandable that she would show women in this way, as everyday she had to arrange the household and she often advised her husband by giving him political advice."

"Do you mean that a woman has to be both educated and homely if she wants to marry into a good family?"

"Err... Yes." Cai Han replied hesitantly.

"I don't like that." She said and ran to her chamber. It was the first time that she realised that it was hard to be a woman. A woman's fate was sealed from the beginning. However, she was not going to yield to fate. She was going to challenge it.

Despite Wenji disliking Ban Zhao's message, Ban Zhao became her idol. Ban Zhao was the prime example of who she wanted to be, a woman well-educated and well known within the dynasty. Cai Wenji knew that it was an extraordinary achievement for Ban Zhao to have finished her brother's writing of the dynasty's history. It was rare to find a female historian, either in the past or during the present. She became determined to read as many historical books as possible in the hopes that one day she could help her father with his history work.

Cai Han was not only a scholar, but also a musician. He had become expert at playing the Guqin (an ancient Chinese musical instrument).

The Guqin was considered an important instrument for high ranking (male) officials of ancient China to master. Can Han was well known for his unparalleled ability.

Before the Han dynasty, the Guqin had just five strings, which allowed five notes to be played: gong (do), shang (re), jiao (mi), hui (so), yu (la). During the Han dynasty, two extra strings were added. According to the *Classic of Music*, gong (do) is the most important note of all, as it represents the emperor. Shang (re) represents officials in the court, jiao (mi) represents people, hui (so) important events, and yu (la) all material objects. These five notes were created based on what astrologists observed in the twenty-eight constellations. Gong notes were the eight in the middle of twenty-eight constellations. According to *The Art of War* by Sun Zi, there should be no more than five musical notes. The gong note was in the middle, with the lowest vibration. Shang notes vibrated a little higher than gong. Jiao notes were used to show that the people were prospering and flourishing. Hui notes meant that everything in the universe was prospering and blooming. Yu notes meant that the whole dynasty would be held as a sacrifice to God in order to celebrate good times. The five notes were deeply connected with the five elements in ancient China. The gong was related to the earth element, shang to gold, jiao to wood, hui to fire, and yu to water.

㇀ ㇀ ㇀ ㇀ ㇀ ㇀

One day, Cai Han was struggling to focus on his reading, as he was deeply worried about the turmoil of the Han dynasty. The court ignored his wisdom, and the emperor would not listen to him. Corrupt officials never stopped raising causing chaos. Loyal officials were persecuted and killed. Cai Han felt helpless in the face of declining standards, unable to wisely influence the course of events. Feeling melancholy and indignant, he started to play the Guqin. Perhaps he used too much nervous tension because a string broke, producing a sharp note.

It was at that moment that Wenji walked into her father's study. When she heard her father playing, she stopped, too fascinated and transfixed to move. Why was father's music so sad? As she heard the string break and the sharp note, Wenji felt a pang of remorse.

"Father," Wenji pushed the door open and entered the room. "I heard you playing. I could not help but hear that discordant sound. It seems a string broke? Was it the second string?" Cai Wenji looked at her father and waited for acknowledgement. She was happy to show off some of her knowledge.

Cai Han, dispelling his concerns, smiled kindly at his child, "What did you say?"

"Was it the second string that broke?"

Surprised, Cai Han looked down at his Guqin and saw that she was right! What a wonderful ear for sound she had, or was it just a lucky guess?

"Yes, the second string has broken." Cai Han said with false calm, "Do you like the music of this instrument?"

Wenji nodded her head.

As he replaced the string he said, "I'll play another piece for you to see if you like it."

Cai Wenji nodded her head with focused attention. This time Cai Han deliberately broke the fourth string, and ceased playing.

"Father, the fourth string just broke."

She was right again! Cai Han marvelled. He could not help being surprised, so he asked, "How do you know which string is broken?"

"I often listen to you playing behind the door. I can easily distinguish the differences between each note."

Cai Han suddenly felt proud. As he found himself less busy than usual, he decided to teach Wenji how to play the Guqin. Traditionally, this instrument was only be played by men, but he was not worried about this rule.

From then on, Wenji learned many famous stories about the Guqin from her father and her own private reading. One of these stories included the legend of the piece *High Mountains and Flowing Water,* a solo piece well-known by the Chinese people. Wenji devoted herself to studying historical books. When she was tired, the music of *High Mountains and Flowing Water* flowed through her fingers. She could not help but picture the images of the beautiful stories that happened many years ago, when Bo Yazi played the music to his young friend Zhong Ziqi. Zhong Ziqi was attentive to the music and commented that the music was aiming at high mountains. Bo Yazi played another tune, aimed at flowing water. Zhong Ziqi said, "You were aiming at the flowing water." The soul mates parted after this brief encounter. Bo Yazi returned to the town where he worked, but remembered his brief encounter with Zhong Ziqi every day. He decided to end his official life earlier than normal and return to Zhong Ziqi's hometown, only to receive the news that Zhong Ziqi was dead. The country folks told Bo Yazi that in order please him, Zhong Ziqi had devoted himself to studying. He wished to pass the Imperial exam and enter into officialdom himself, but he had sadly died of hunger.

Hearing this news, Bo Yazi smashed his favourite Guqin to pieces and never played again. Good music always needs a good story.

Though Wenji was young, she could not but feel there was an empty space in the bottom of her heart. She longed to find a soul mate who would understand her. The Guqin had become a tool for her to express herself, and under the careful guidance of her father she gained considerable expertise from a young age. Wenji's favourite note in Guqin was 'jiao', the note that represented the wood element and which told stories of common people.

What a life it was to be a young lady, already worrying about her future!

Chapter Two

The vicissitudes of Cai Wenji's teenage life

Wenji grew up with grace and elegance, with music and books for company. If one would compare her to a flower, she would be a white peony, graceful and beautiful. She was slender, and when she walked she resembled a willow blowing in the breeze. She was intelligent and strong-willed, but not rebellious. She was proud, even though she had not yet reached adulthood. Her beautiful eyes shone brightly, like pair of moonstones.

Wenji was a far sighted young woman, even if she was just a teenage girl. She longed to travel and see the beautiful sights of mountains, rivers, forests, and the vast sea. *Wisdom in hold, elegance in mould. This ancient saying reflects the inner confidence Wenji possessed,* drawing a link between her education and class. However, for now she had to be satisfied with the pictures she conjured in her mind.

She was obsessed with music, losing herself in the sentiment of the tunes she played. She could not help feeling sensitive and sad. She heard the terrible news of the termination of her father's official position. Wenji was perceptive enough to be aware of the gap between reality and dreams. She despaired that the sole goal of the common people was survival. Wenji wanted to be a woman like Ban Zhao, so that she would have a chance to help her father create the historical record. Fate can sometimes be cruel.

However, the destiny of the country rises and falls, falls and then rises. The four seasons circle to be reborn. People had fallen in love with each other, hated each other, and parted from each other, as if strangers.

The kingdom was divided by different warlords, and would one day be united by the strongest and cleverest leader. Wenji was not as lucky as Ban Zhao, but heroes and heroines always appear in troubled times. The emperor of Eastern Han dynasty preferred earthly pleasures to matters of state. He gradually began to ignore the political affairs of the dynasty, spending his days singing and dancing with his concubines. Cai Han remonstrated with the emperor many times, but this only annoyed the emperor. The corrupt officials turned on and slandered Cai Han. Concocted charges were levied against him. The emperor was quite happy to hear these charges against Cai Han, as Cai Han's truth was not what the emperor wanted to hear. The emperor had longed wanted an excuse to expel Cai Han from the court, so the emperor was only too glad to hold these ridiculous and unfounded charges against him. Cai Han said in a deeply anguished voice, "My lord, heaven is witness to my loyalty to the Eastern Han dynasty. I would rather die in front of you than to see the dynasty ruined by your hands! Lord... Do you have any idea of what transpires in your kingdom? Do you still think it is the same Han dynasty it was before? If you were to venture out of the palace, you will see people starving on the streets. You will see houses lying in ruin. You will hear of the corrupt officials who impose harsh laws on farmers. Homeless children are begging in the street. These same rich and corrupt officials are waving rain and blood! My dear Lord! I stand on my reputation that if I ever did something against law, or bully the poor people, I would rather die in the court." Following these words, Cai Han was about to take his place in the rear of the court, but he was stopped by his colleagues. At this crucial moment, almost the entire gathering knelt down and kowtowed to the emperor, said as one, "Please, Lord! We know that Cai Han is not guilty. He has devoted his life to the Han dynasty. Proof of his sterling effort and contribution is evidenced everywhere. His contribution to building the historic literature of the Han dynasty is extraordinary. Throughout history, a gentlemen such as he could never win the approval of corrupt officials, because he exposes them. Please Lord; don't listen to gossip or slander. Open your eyes soberly and pick up your ears to hear. Reconsider your judgment one more time."

Cai Han was overwhelmed and his eye brimmed with tears. He was deeply touched by his colleagues who tried to save his life at the risk of losing their own.

Seeing and hearing this from so many in the court, the muddle-headed emperor felt pressured and, in the end, said nothing. Then a thought dawned on him - he became suspicious and wondered if Cai Han had not organised this clique to pursue his own selfish interests. Why did so many officials speak for his sake? Stupid emperor! He was an emperor who wore no clothes – but no one dared to point out the truth to him, except Cai Han. However, this uprightness also brought troubles to Cai Han. It was a well-known saying that good medicine, though bitter in taste, was able to cure illness; honest advice was unpleasant to hear. What they said of Cai Han touched the emperor's guilt. He was aware that things in the kingdom were not good, but he deceived himself as if nothing had changed, so as to continue his life of excess. Yes, he was running away from reality, but every time he met Cai Han he would have to face that reality, which made the emperor squirm. But now all the officials in the court were kneeling down and speaking for Cai Han's sake – what to do? Certainly, he could not lose face in the court, as he had already announced Cai Han's guilt. He would not cry over spilt milk.

Yes, Cai Han's influence in the court and his reputation were too large to ignore. The emperor was conscious of the weight of Cai Han's words. He was aware that if Cai Han was dead, many would rebel and accuse him of stupidity. He was aware of the decline of his dynasty... it was unavoidable. He was aware that the different warlords were dividing up the kingdom and were ruling in their own name. The emperor considered Cai Han and his reputation as a threat. The emperor still pondered. The court was quiet, waiting.

Suddenly, the emperor burst out laughing in this awkward atmosphere, "My dear fellows please get up!" Then addressing Cai Han he pronounced, "Out of consideration for your years of diligent effort to serve the kingdom, I will free you from the death sentence. But you are to be banished from the capital, together with your family. You are to go to the border of the far North Frontier".

There was a low hum as the news was received. This was the border with the Hun Kingdom, and was considered the coldest and most distant place, a purgatory of sorts. The people of the Hun Kingdom were considered barbarians. To be outcast as such was to be separated from all that was good.

ㄱ ㄱ ㄱ ㄱ ㄱ

In this way, Cai Han's life was saved. Without complaint, he and his family started the journey towards the cold north. They took the family coach, but had to take turns walking, as there was not enough room for them all and the small amount of luggage they took. The coach was unpleasant to sit in as it rocked over the bumpy road.

The weather became colder the further north they travelled. They felt like outcasts, unknown by the local people they passed. Along the way, they crossed vast areas of cold deserts, swamps, and gloomy forests. It was a miserable journey, during which they enduring many hardships.

Never during this harsh time did Wenji complain. She clearly understood what it meant for her and her family to be expelled to the edge of the world. Her ambitions, dreams and plans had disintegrated. Her care-free-past was gone, forever! She was immersed in a deep sorrow, just as the other members of her family were. However, seeing the suffering of the common people, Wenji forgot her sorrow and did what she could to help them. Her troubles were mild compared to these poor wretches. She wondered, what was the use of jewels, banquets, servants or reputations, when life itself was so precarious? These things were just like flowers in the mirror, or the moon on the water – only decorations that could not save people's lives.

Wenji only took her Guqin and a few favourite books as luggage, knowing she had to be practical. She needed to survive! As far as she could see, her future life would be full of endless troubles and obstacles. There was nothing sadder than seeing her once prosperous family declining at such a young age – a trauma for her young heart. Everything had changed in her life and she knew she had to be strong and clever in order to survive in these troubled times.

ㄱ ㄱ ㄱ ㄱ ㄱ

It took the family over a month before they arrived at their outpost. Throughout the journey, Wenji took note of the landscape they travelled through. It was by this lucky — or unlucky coincidence — that Wenji, who was once a spoiled princess, was forced to traverse the country and see what the world really looked like! What she saw was poverty, hunger, disease and death. It was a time when plague ravaged the poor. She knew the rich robbed the poor in order to increase their own wealth. They wasted money and locked themselves up in their golden palaces, the poor dying at their door. She also saw the beauty of the country, its solitude. She witnessed indigo mountains at sunset, and vast planes that stretched as far as the eye could see. On that journey she became a Child of China, and these experiences would be reflected in her later compositions.

가 가 가 가 가

When Cai Han's family finally arrived, they sat in the coach and surveyed the shabby cottage that was to be their home. It was not even in the town, but rather was situated in the countryside. Wenji could not help feeling disappointed, but her sorrows quickly vanished when she saw her father trying to remain in high spirits. Wenji's mother assured Cai Han that living in such a cottage, at the feet of the great mountain of Wangwu (one China's most famous mountains) and close to the Yellow River, was auspicious.

Living in the great valley at the foot of Wangwu Mountain would enable them to fully enjoy the pleasures of being 'free people', who would be able to plant crops in the field to support their living. But, as the north was bitterly cold, they would find it difficult to grow crops.

Fortunately, they still had a few servants, the rest of whom had been left behind. Upon entering the cottage, the furniture was scarce and worn. There was an old cupboard, a small rustic kitchen, and a bed. Still, they would make the best of it and be a family. Looking on the positive side, Wenji knew she would be able to continue her love affair with the Guqin.

As it turned out, the music helped her sanity. Whenever she touched the Guqin, she felt all her troubles fall away.

Now Wenji had to adapt to life without a personal servant. She did this in as cheerful a way as possible, so as to help her parents.

She would not be crushed by bitterness for this harshness that had been thrust upon them. It was almost by remaining positive and happy that she would spite the emperor. It was rare for a young lady of such breeding to never shed a tear in such circumstances. She acted bravely, pretending to be cheerful and joked with her father about their misfortunes.

She showed great filial piety to her mother, trying to make her happy. And so, in this small cottage, there was sometimes laughter.

However, when alone, Wenji was fully absorbed by her music and inner thoughts. She could not help but wonder whether it was wiser to act like an irresponsible person, devoted to drink, playing music, and pretending that there was nothing wrong in this turbulent world – or to be sober to reality, to criticise everything and grumble at the unfairness of fate. What is the use of being as sober as her father? It seemed that the wicked always won over the good. No justice would be done in a troubled society.

Often, Wenji listened to the music coming from her father's room, and wondered why her father was too stubborn to remonstrate with that foolish puppy emperor, and instead chose to be quiet out of self-protection?

$$\text{弓 弓 弓 弓 弓}$$

Two long years had passed since the family moved to the North Frontier. Few visitors came because of the remoteness of the cottage. They also did not want to be associated with the 'outcasts'. Again, Wenji used these quiet times to further educate herself, and practice the Guqin.

She tried to understand and feel the music, but she found that the strings would often break. For a time she would give up, but she always returned to the instrument and tried to play the most difficult Guqin pieces. She did not want to accept that perhaps she was still too young to understand the music.

One day, after Wenji and her mother had prepared the evening meal for her father, she spoke. There was a question that had been troubling her and that made her restless. She hesitated before quickly saying, "Father, I have a question for you."

"Please!" His father sipped his tea and wondered what whim his daughter had in her mind this time.

It was a moment of weakness for Wenji, whose eyes showed concern. "Why didn't that stupid emperor follow your advice and instead drive you from the capital? Don't they know what good you did for the Kingdom, and that what you asked for was based on your loyalty to the emperor?"

Cai Han could not help the sad smile that appeared on his face, and he sighed deeply. He never expected that a young lady would have such thoughts. Looking at his only child, he was shocked to realise how deep an impact his demotion had had on his daughter. He had to make her realise that she had to come out from the golden fairy tale world of her past, and face brutal reality. What had happened was beyond their control, they had to adapt.

"Ha, you can be another Ban Zhao, even better than her, but in a different way." Her father's smile reassured her, "Ban Zhao was quite lucky to be born in the peaceful times of Han dynasty, but you live in a troubled time. Who knows how destiny plays its cards?"

Her eyebrows knitted together, "Why can't the Han dynasty keep on rising forever?" Her resentment at the unfair treatment her family suffered erupted like a volcano. The carefree girl of the past had gone forever! Indeed, what she foresaw along the road was hunger and poverty, in this icy wilderness. The harsh reality had eaten her up. Why was life so cruel?

"It's okay." Cai Han was surprised at his daughter's violent emotions. He wanted Cai Wenji to understand that sometimes it is better to face your fears. So he continued, "It's quite natural. Life is full of ups and downs... Today it is a sunny day, but you can't be sure of rain tomorrow. If you threw a stone up, the stone can never go up forever, in the end it has to fall to the ground. If you want the stone to keep going upwards, you must pick it up and throw it again. The stone doesn't move in a straight line, but rather in a curve, with its highest point in the middle, but a low point in the beginning and end. If the emperor's eyes choose not to see, his ears not to hear, then the fate of whole Kingdom declines".

Wenji nodded her head. "Father, shall we stay here forever?"

"I don't know. We will wait and see." Cai Han smiled and continued, "No one can ever foresee what will happen. Do you think the north is too horrible to live in? Feel the beating pulse of nature here, you can find out its surprises! As it is cold, even in the summer, there aren't many guests to bother us. We can live a life of freedom. There is always hope." Cai Han looked at his daughter thoughtfully, "Promise me that in the future, whatever happens, you will keep on living and adapting to the situation. Try every means to survive, even if you are living in continuous difficulty. Do you understand?"

Wenji could not help but burst into tears. She did not want to believe the world was so dark. But she muttered her assent, "Father, I promise to be strong".

Cai Han nodded his head in satisfaction.

习 习 习 习 习

It was well said that we can never know what life is to bring us. Misfortune follows fortune. The warlord Dong Zhuo of the Eastern Han was gaining the upper hand, expanding his influence over the royal family and civilians.

The foolish emperor, who was addicted to sloth and seduction, regretted the weakening of his power and the strengthening of Dong Zhuo's. He realised what a fool he was to dismiss the wise council of Cai Han. But now it was too late. If only he could turn back time, he would never make the same stupid mistake again!

The emperor saw Dong Zhuo as just another warlord who wanted to control him and give orders. The only problem for Dong Zhuo was that he lacked the legitimacy to become emperor, as there was no royal blood in his veins.

In order to strengthen his control over the emperor, Dong Zhuo sought out the wise and influential men throughout the realm, and as he did, he gained even greater control. Cai Han, of course was on his list.

Dong Zhuo himself travelled to Cai Han's shabby cottage in the north. Upon his arrival, Cai Han was shocked to see this official and warlord at his door after so many years.

"Cai Han, you must return to the capital and help me restore the glory of Han dynasty. Will you come?"

Cai Han was astute and judged Dong Zhuo as not being a worthy man to follow. To save face on Dong Zhuo's behalf, with a trembling voice Cai Han said, "I am too old."

"You are needed. Honoured Cai, you are a great scholar and I need you." Then he chuckled and took out his sword, placing it on the table. "You will follow me back to the capital, and serve the emperor wholeheartedly. In return, I will give you great fortune and guarantee the safety of your family. Refuse and you will shake hands with my sword!"

Cai Han knew he had no choice but to return to the capital. He had to put the safety of his family first. Moreover, it was not for the sake of money or fame, but for the sake of saving the dynasty.

Dong Zhuo ordered a very luxurious coach to bring Cai's family back to the capital. Quite unexpectedly, upon returning to the capital, he received great respect from Dong Zhuo, who promoted him to the position of duke in the town of Gao Yang. The Cai family returned in glory. They had moved into a bigger residence than before. The ostentation and extravagance were beyond measure.

Dong Zhuo wanted the whole world to see how much he valued the erudite and talented scholar Cai Han. Wenji saw her past of carefree days and luxury return.

The stupid emperor could achieve nothing without Dong Zhuo's advice! It was the emperor who had driven all the talented officials away, but Dong Zhuo recalled them. Dong Zhuo manipulated the emperor to rule the country. Only he, the great Dong Zhuo, could bring justice and glory to the realm. He would be respected.

The fact remained however that in those troubled times, no one in his position would be safe forever. The direction of the wind changed whenever and wherever. In 192 AD another warlord named Wang Yun used a series of tricks and strategies to drive a wedge between Dong Zhuo and his son Lu Bu. In his anger, Lu Bu killed Dong Zhuo, presumably for the sake of a beautiful woman that both father and son had fallen in love with. When the news came to the ears of the common citizens, they clapped their hands and cheered.

Cai Han was not pleased, as it was Dong Zhuo who had resurrected his life and influence. He was loyal to him. Loyalty was an important trait for scholars, especially in troubled times.

Cai Han's pity for Dong Zhuo's death reached Wang Yun's ears. Wang Yun was another loyal official of the Han dynasty. However, he had always been jealous of Cai Han. When he heard that Cai Han showed pity towards Dong Zhuo publicly, he reported this to the emperor, accusing Cai Han of confusing his allegiance to Dong Zhuo with that of the emperor. Cai Han was again sentenced to jail, and, thereafter, death.

Cai Han wrote to Wang Yun to ask for leniency, stating that he was willing to accept the punishment of cutting off his two feet in order to gain time to finish writing the records of the Han dynasty.

Wang Yun declined his request. Cai Han regretted his narrow mindedness, but it was already too late. Later, in a twist of irony, Wang Yun was also murdered by troops loyal to Dong Zhuo.

Cai Han was executed at the age of sixty.

When the news of her father's death reached Wenji, it was as if a lightning bolt had pierced her heart. Sadness overwhelmed her – but she did not break. She spent hours playing the Guqin, where her unbounded sorrow infiltrated the strings. She could now play the most difficult music with ease.

Wenji was now a young lady. She had book learning, played the Guqin excellently, and was intelligent, witty, and easy going. She was also graced with beautiful looks. She moved with the ease of a swan gliding over water. Her bright eyes were not overshadowed by the sorrows that she had experienced. Her manners and etiquette were always graceful. However, she was more realistic about material life after her time in the North Frontier.

Now that Wenji was of age, her mother, Zhao Wuniang (who was also well-educated) made the decision to marry Wenji to Wei Zhongdao to help overcome the catastrophes that had befallen the family. As it happened, it was a good match for Wenji, as Zhongdao, the only son of a well-to-do family, was also scholarly inclined.

Wei Zhongdao was an understanding and caring man. He was tall, thin, and carried the hunched shoulders of a scholar. He had a pleasant face, with dark eyes and thick eyebrows. A gentleman with impeccable manners, he delivered his words softly and with care. Never, though, could he have been thought of as a warrior.

He had long heard of the beauty and intelligence of Wenji, so the marriage was likely to satisfy him. They married quickly because of the political troubles that were imminent.

Once married, he loved Wenji wholeheartedly. Wenji though, still felt sorrow over the death of her father. But in time Zhongdao's love melted the icy shadows in her heart, and soon she was in love for the first time in her life. Zhongdao and Wenji were a suitable match. Both of them were born into elite families, where wealth and education were plentiful.

Yet, Wenji mourned her father and lacked the spontaneity of a new wife. Zhongdao was attentive, and instructed the servant to prepare Wenji's breakfast and deliver it to her every day. He told her that there was no need to perform formalities for his parents. Wenji was grateful, as it was in the morning when she missed her father the most. She would look at Zhongdao with watery eyes, and say, "Thank you." These two words were enough for Zhongdao, who was sensitive to her feelings. Embarrassed, he said that there was no need for thanks. But she still shed silent tears whenever she thought of her father's death, and she could not consummate the marriage.

引 引 引 引 引

Normally in the mornings she stayed in her room reading, but early one spring morning, when peach flowers filled the courtyard and the air smelled sweet, she went out to embrace spring. The pink flowers proudly blossomed under the bright sunlight. Wenji wandered through the garden to a large pond. The water was clear, and fish could be seen at the bottom. Wenji decided to stroll up to the pavilion on the small hill. When she got there, she surveyed the garden. For the moment she could let go of her sorrows. She sat in the pavilion for a long time, embracing the fresh spring air. Looking around, she was reminded of the marvellous creations of nature. Wenji heard flowing water below the pavilion, and heard the chirping of birds, who also seemed to be enjoying spring. Life was reborn. She recalled the words of her father, and how right he was. She had a yearning to play music and called for her maid to bring her Guqin. She put the Guqin on the stone table and began to play "*Flowing water*" to express her deep admiration towards nature.

The music drifted across the yard. Entranced, Zhongdao emerged from his study to follow the music. He had never heard her play and was mesmerised by the sound of her music. Dazzled, it seemed as if an angel had occupied the pavilion. Her sleeves fluttered in the breeze. Her face was angelic, focused, and unaware of his arrival. He said nothing as he did not want to break the spell. When she finished, he applauded and asked his servant to bring his Guqin. He asked her to again play *Flowing water* and he started to play *High Mountain*. The sound of the two songs played together was bewitching. In that moment, they were one, the same vibration, of one heartbeat, love made manifest through sound. Each stopped, to listen to the other. Bees and butterflies were attracted to the sounds and fluttered around them. Peach petals floated off trees in melodic harmony towards the ground. The servants ceased their work and silently gathered around to listen. They smiled at each other, their eyes transfixed on the graceful couple. They wondered whether these two were a god and goddess from a fairy tale.

Wenji's heart was overwhelmed with wave after wave of warmth mixed with shyness as she watched Zhongdao serenade her with his musical instrument.

When they finished, they sat stunned, staring into the other's eyes. In the full witness of his servants, Zhongdao crossed to his wife and affectionately hugged her before slowly walking back down the hill to his office and work.

殳 殳 殳 殳 殳

Wei Zhongdao's mother, Shang Weihong, despised Wenji. At first she was happy for her son to marry, but then jealousy set in. She was jealous of Wenji's good looks, her intellect, and the fact that her son spent all his spare time with Wenji. She witnessed the two playing the Guqin together in the pavilion. She was not romanced as the servants had been.

That evening, in the privacy of their room, Zhongdao put his arms around his wife's slender waist. Wenji no longer resisted and laid her head on his shoulder. She listened to her husband's heartbeat, and remembered when their hearts beat as one earlier in the pavilion. Zhongdao stroked her soft hair. For the first time in her life, she knew the pleasure of a man and love.

When their lovemaking was exhausted, slightly breathless, she became aware of the sweet smell of his body. "Why does your body smell so sweet?"

He chuckled, "You must be joking... Come, it's time to get up." Wenji held him, "Don't, not yet". A poem had come to her:

By the river, lush reeds grow, covered with dew.
My beauty, in my mind, why are you standing at the
other side of river?
I wade upstream to find you, but it is far and distant.
I wade downwards towards you, still,
with many obstacles.

When finished she frowned. He smiled, "I am by your side. There's no need to worry." He then asked, "Which poem from the *Book of Songs* do you like the most?"

Wenji said without pausing to think, "*If you give me a peach, I will return with a pear.*"

He replied, "So, if I love you wholeheartedly? What are you going to give me in return?"

"I will offer you my tears." Wenji joked light-heartedly.

He frowned, "I don't want you to be sad. What do you think of this poem? *When I met you in the wind and storms, how could I conceal the happiness in my heart*? Do you like it?"

"Oh, No! You have asked for too much. I can't tell a lie, *I can only part with you when the mountain has eroded to nothing; when the sky and earth have become one; when thunder in the spring becomes so astonishing; and in the summer snow falls."*

"Why not? I like to hear your lies."

刾 刾 刾 刾 刾

Life is so short and beautiful moments come and go in the blink of an eye. The newly married couples' happiness did not last. In just one year, Wei Zhongdao was diagnosed with a serious illness. Wenji was distraught. She approached every doctor in the region, but all of them said her husband's disease was incurable.

One day, when Wenji was issuing medicine to Zhongdao, one spoon after another, Zhongdao suddenly grabbed her hands and said with laboured determination, "I'm dying. I know it."

"No, don't say such words. I will spend all our money to employ the best doctors to cure you."

"No, it's a waste of time. I'd rather you be with me as much as possible." With a faint smile he continued, "I never knew what happiness was until I met you. I will die without regret."

He clutched Wenji's hands tightly and whispered his love for her. Soon thereafter, with a smile still on his lips, his eyes slowly closed, and he died.

At first Wenji thought he had lapsed into sleep, but when she felt the body grow cold her tears and hysteria had no limits. So tragic was the scene that that even the sparrows flew away. She felt robbed, Wei Zhongdao was so young, and she had become a widow in her twentieth summer. It was then that she recalled the prophetic words of her favourite poem, and what they truly meant.

刾 刾 刾 刾 刾

Cai Wenji did not shed a single tear when the coffin was placed in the ground, as all her tears had already dried up. To make matters worse, Wenji's mother-in-law now regarded Cai Wenji as a bad omen, and began to treat her badly. She believed it was Wenji who had bewitched Zhongdao and dried out his blood.

Zhongdao's mother instructed Wenji to do servant's work. She had little time to read, write or play music. How could Wenji, a proud and arrogant young lady, bear this humiliation?

One day, after she had finished her work and was lost in remorse, Wenji decided to sit down to play the Guqin. Her mother-in-law burst in, hurling a torrent of abuse, "How dare you play such music after my son's death? Don't you know it is your very existence that caused his end? Since you arrived, what have you brought to the family? Nothing! Only death and unhappiness. I regret agreeing to the marriage between you and my son, especially as you are the daughter of a shameless official who lost his reputation."

Wenji's hands trembled in anger. Her mother-in-law was free to humiliate her if she wanted, but what right did she have to point her finger at her dear father?

Wenji immediately made up her mind and said decisively in her soft voice, "Seeing as you hate me so much, I will leave." With these words she walked out of the room, and went to her own room to pack her belongings.

Seeing Wenji so controlled and firm, her mother-in-law lost her temper and threw Wenji's books to the floor as she shouted loudly, "Get out of here, you wicked girl! You whore! You don't care about your reputation! Just get out of here with your dirty musical instrument and books."

These insults just added further injury to Wenji's already broken heart. In just a few years, she not only lost her father, but also her husband. Although Wenji seemed to take it bravely, inside she was crumbling. It seemed that misfortune was part of her life. Holding back tears, she held her Guqin tightly in her arms, and left the room, with the mother-in-law shouting at her back. Without a backward glance, Wenji ignored the abuse, and slammed the door behind her.

Saddened and scared, Wenji finished collected her belongings. Several times she passed by her mother-in-law's room, but her mother-in-law did not once raise her head. When she had all that she could carry, Wenji walked out of the house. She hesitated in front of the gate, looking back at the room where she and her husband had made love. If only things had been different, she thought to herself. Then she turned around and walked away.

Chapter Three

Life in the Northern Frontier again

Wenji's mother, Wuniang, was shocked by her daughter's sudden arrival back at the family home in the capital. According to the customs of the Eastern Han dynasty, when a woman married she became the property of her husband's family. It was forbidden for her to return to her mother's house or marry again. It would be considered virtuous that a young twenty-year-old girl like Wenji should remain a widow in her mother-in-law's home for the rest of her life.

Wenji's mother picked up a broom from the corner of the room and angrily hit Wenji. She shouted at her, "How could you be so selfish as to leave your mother-in-law in her time of mourning? Are you not mourning for your dead husband? Don't you know how the world is going to judge you? People will humiliate you as a dissolute woman. By being married you don't belong here anymore. Don't you know the rules of society?"

Wenji tried to avoid being hit but was resolute, "No, I will not go back. I would rather stay here and take your beating than go back to that witch."

Her mother shouted back, "You are inconsiderate! How dare you say those words?" As she did, she slapped her daughter across the face.

"I did nothing wrong. I could not stay there; the Wei family are too cold. It was hell, she hated me from the time I met my husband." She searched her mother's eyes for signs of sympathy, while hers were flooded with tears. "Mother, am I not your child? Are you willing to see me endure a painful life in that soulless house, all alone? Should I stay there to suffer humiliation at the hands of that old–" Wenji was about to curse, but she stopped herself.

Her mother said an anguished voice, "Child, you bring shame to our family! I am feeling giddy, and must lie down." She staggered out of the room.

Wenji was appalled by her mother's attitude. Why did she not understand? It would seem that the vicissitudes of life would not stop. Her husband was dead, her father was dead, her mother-in-law hated her, and now her mother was abandoning her. Why did they all say that she brought shame to the family? Why should she obey custom and allow her young life to go to waste by endlessly mourning and waiting?

Wenji's sadness was constant, like waves battering the sea shore. Now she alone she tried to maintain her calm, but her body shivered from anger and despair. Listless, she wandered from room to room.

Later, when she went to rest in her chamber, she saw that all was the same as before. Everything was so familiar – the dusty books on the shelf, the bed and the decorations. She remembered the happy memories she had made here, like practicing Guqin and reading. It was from this room that she would peek out to see her father's visitors. They were sophisticated and worldly. She was always filled with curiosity and wanted to know what they talked about. Among her father's many guests, one left a deep impression on her. His name was Cao Cao. Once when she asked her father, "Who was that man?" he replied, "That was Cao Cao, a hero from the troubled times." Since then, Wenji would stare in awe at Cao Cao each time he came. Hidden, with the door only opened a crack, she studied his every move. She thought him handsome, with an air of worldliness.

Now, looking around her room, it upset her to think that this was the same place, yet so much had changed.

习 习 习 习 习

Later, Wuniang left her daughter and went to her husband's tombstone to seek consolation and clarity. It was the first time she had hit Wenji so remorselessly, and now she felt anxious and confused. She blamed herself for not educating her daughter well enough in traditional customs. It was bad enough before, but now with this stain on her character, and the anger of her-mother-in law, it was too much. She would be an outcast from society, a source of gossip.

Zhao Wuniang lit the joss sticks that were used to worship family ancestors. She whispered to her husband's soul and asked with anguish, "Why did you pass away so young, and abandon us? I am so sorry... I tried my best to educate our daughter, but it was in vain, she is so headstrong. It was I who arranged the marriage for her into that well-to-do family! Wenji was happy with the marriage, but why did her husband die after just one year of marriage? The girl is distraught, and now she is behaving unreasonably." As she spoke, memories of her husband rushed through her mind. She thought of their wedding, how she gave birth to Wenji, the sudden fall of Cai Han's career, Wenji's hurried betrothal, Cai Han being sentenced to jail, and his death. Suddenly, she was feeling very old. She could not bear such a turbulent life. She once had dreams. She dreamed that the world was safe, and her husband would stay in his position forever. There would be status and pride. She dreamed of harmony and that they would live in peace. However, her sorrows wiped away everything that was beautiful – now all was ugly. Her beloved husband was no longer at her side and her daughter was without virtue. With these thoughts, her vision suddenly swirled. It was all too much for her, and she felt a sudden stab of pain in her heart. Her vision blurred, and she fell unconscious on her husband's tombstone.

Wenji found her mother slumped over her father's tombstone. She hurriedly called for a doctor, but after feeling for Wuniang's pulse, the doctor shook his head. With pity in his voice, he told Wenji that it was too late – her mother had passed away.

ㄱ ㄱ ㄱ ㄱ ㄱ

Wenji, barely an adult, was totally alone, without parents, a husband, or siblings. Seeing her mother's body lying motionless on the ground, she was numb. No thought entered her mind, her stare was blank. It was only later that she wondered what was to become of her. At just twenty years old, already a widow and an orphan, she had experienced more than most women did in their entire lives. Clever as she was, she had no way to understand her situation or cope with yet another shock. God has mocked her, played this ridiculous joke on her! Yet her instincts told her to not give up on living. She felt that she still had too much to offer, too much to accomplish. She briefly remembered her the time in the garden pavilion, where spring had called out to her with its beauty. To live will always be difficult. To die is so simple. She pondered. Although now it seemed to be the winter of her life, she knew spring would come again. She had to find the strength to carry on. It would be hard, but she would first get over the loss of all her loved ones and the loss of her status. Her heart was still beating warmly. She still had some hope for the future.

She inherited her parents' wealth and continued to live in the family home, mourning her parents' death. However, strong as she was, this last death was too much to bear. For months she was lethargic, incapable of reading or writing. She spent her days in bed, and dismissed the servants. One evening, filled with frustration, she suddenly threw off the bedclothes and went to her bookshelf. Here, she tore the book of Ban Zhao into pieces and threw them into the fire. Angrily, she watched the flames flare up, the book reduced to ashes. Helpless, on her own, she lay on the floor, and curled up into the foetal position. She was an empty shell with no hope, no prospects, and no energy. How long she stayed there for — a night, a whole day — she had no idea. All she knew was that she had no one she could rely upon, and all the beautiful things in her life, including her ambition, were destroyed. However, deep within her heart something was still preserved, not just the will to survive, but the need to thrive. Yet, she was not aware of this at that time.

引 引 引 引 引

Over the following months, the fortunes of the dynasty sharply declined. Political turbulence swept the country; warlords provoked war, and the dukes and other powerful families rebelled and occupied territories, claiming them as their own. Many deaths occurred as the vanquished were routinely massacred. The sky was constantly filled with the dust send up by the galloping of many horses. Blood was spilt with ease. The Eastern Han dynasty was so vulnerable that it could collapse with a simple change of the breeze. Crops and homes were burned, and starving people wandered the country in groups, scouring the landscape for anything to eat. Children begged, or lay dead by the roadside. The dynasty was divided by warlords, but none was strong enough to unite the kingdom. The worst was still to come; the Hun Kingdom took advantage of the weakened Han dynasty and invaded.

During the chaos of war, like many others Cai Wenji's home was destroyed and she was forced to lead the life of a vagabond, with hair dishevelled and face dirty, carrying her cherished Guqin and a few of her favourite books. She joined the crowds of people fleeing the capital.

Which direction should she go in? Should she follow the bulk of people heading south? Or following the few who were heading north? Her mind was racing. It occurred to her that she was more familiar with the north than the south, as she had lived in the northern frontier with her family.

She remembered the first time she went to the north five years ago, when she was just a child. Now she was to run away from the city as a refugee. It meant that she had to walk a thousand miles to find the same place, but this time she would be alone. There was enormous danger and hardship ahead of her. She doubted her ability to survive. It was well said that a fallen master was no better than a whore. But she had to keep on going, there was no other choice. Summoning her courage, she headed north. Anyone watching her thin body carrying her burden of her most cherished possessions would not have expected her to get very far. But they could not see the determination that fuelled her. She would cling to whatever hope she had left.

In order to reach the north, she had to pass through the city gates. She covered her face with mud so as not to be recognised by the soldiers. Carrying her Guqin on her back, and with a lowed head, she tried to pass through the gates with the crowds by taking the advantage of turmoil. With her heart pounding in her ears, her ragged but fine clothes and bearing betrayed her. She was stopped by a guard.

"Oh, oh! What a beauty. Well-disguised. Let's clean up your face." The soldier looked Wenji up and down. He acted as if an animal had found its way into his trap. His intentions were obvious; he wanted to rape her.

Facing a crisis, Wenji was able to show her quick wits, "Please, I beg your mercy. I was sick with smallpox." "Smallpox?"

To Wenji's relief the solider hurriedly retreated a few steps away from her. However, his senses quickly returned. He looked Wenji up and down and burst out laughing. "You're lying; I have seen many women who have had smallpox. None of them look like you. It's just mud on your face", he said as his cold thick finger flicked mud from her face, revealing her clear skin.

"What's going on here?" At this moment, the leader of the troop arrived, and began shouting at the soldier.

The leader approached nearer to see what was going on. He saw a lady troubled by his soldier. When his eyes met Wenji's he was stunned. What he saw was an extraordinary beauty with her face covered with mud. The leader could see that she was a lady of good breeding. There was something mysterious in her that attracted him deeply, something far beyond her beauty. Seeing that his soldier showed no respect to this young lady of class, the leader's temper flared.

"I told you many times not to molest young woman or steal from them. Do you not remember your orders?"

"I'm sorry sir. I was just interrogating her." The soldier knelt down, trembling and continued in a shaky voice. "My Tso-hyun, please forgive me. I am willing to die for you a thousand times in the battlefield to atone for my sins".

"Stand up! If you dare disobey this order again, I will punish you according to martial law."

"I will remember."

Tso-hyun turned to Wenji and said, "I'm sorry young lady. This ordeal must have been a shock to you. Our soldiers are in need of discipline, their manners quite rude. Would you like some refreshment?"

Wenji looked up and saw a strong masculine face studying her. She could not help but look into in his deep, powerful eyes. She saw her own reflection and felt her heart flutter. In a daze, she could sense the strength of this man. She had no choice but to be led away by him and let events unfold as they would.

The junior solder spat to the ground, thinking that the commander only wanted to take the girl for himself. He felt like a fox that had lost its meal.

Inside the commander's tent it was warm, and she soon stopped shivering. She was conscious that the man was of high rank. He had a broad forehead and a muscular figure. She could not help blushing and felt awkward. Then she had the realisation, the man was a foreigner, from a different ethnic group. Wenji noticed the silver sword hanging on his waist. His was cleanly dressed and well-groomed. He was in his prime, aged somewhere between twenty-five and thirty.

This was Wenji's first time in the tent of a Hun. She looked around and saw that the tent was round, a yurt. It seemed small outside, but was spacious inside. Both the wall and the floor were covered with beautiful, richly-woven carpets. They were embroidered with many animals worshipped by the Hun, like eagles and wolves. The carpets felt soft on her feet, as if she was standing on a soft animal fur.

Her host invited her to sit on the carpet and offered her a hand warmer, which she gladly took and put her hands inside. He called out to a servant and spoke to them for moment, before turning back to watch her scan his yurt with interest. A short while later, milk tea with brown rice was served. Tso-hyun poured the tea in an exquisite, delicate red cup, which he offered to Wenji. She quickly sipped without a thank you. It warmed her body. It tasted was salty, sweet and strong at the same time, very different to the tea she drank at home.

By way of conversation, he told her that he is a commander in the army of the Hun King, and that that he owned a large amount of land in the Hun territory. He also had a minor title. Although she tried to hide it, she let out a sigh. He noticed with surprised and asked her gently, "What is your name?"

"Can Yan, but my nickname is named Wenji." She replied.

He thought for a moment before saying, "Ah… are you the daughter of the famous scholar Cai Han?" Tso-hyun immediately stood up, his eyes shining with wolfish excitement.

"Yes." Wenji said flatly. The name no longer resonated with her.

"Oh, how lucky for me! I don't believe it was just coincidence that we met in this place at this moment, where thousands pass by this gate daily. Destiny! In my wildest dream, I could never have expected to encounter the daughter of the well-respected and famous scholar, Cai Han. What an honour for me to invite you for refreshment." It was clear that he was entranced by her. "A few minutes ago, I was just wondering who this fine looking young lady who stood out among the crowd could be. What's the use of putting mud on your face? You would still stand out even if you dressed in beggar's clothes and coloured your face. I have discovered a treasure!"

Wenji had calmed down and was now studying Tso-hyun. The man in front of her, foreign as he was, aroused mixed feelings in her, including doubt, shame, and intrigue. But she had no idea of his intent. He seemed to be a gentleman. He ended her speculation, "The war is over. I'm to take my troops back to our home in the Hun North. Will you come with me? You are alone, and it's dangerous for a lady to journey alone…" He abruptly stopped as she stared at the floor. He could see she was conflicted, her head spinning with a thousand thoughts. *Would she be safe doing this? What if her people pointed their fingers to her and called her a traitor!* She looked up and searched his face for a sign. He continued, "I will see that you are protected, and will provide you with everything you need. Forgive me for being blunt, but I am a warrior and know of no other way. I know that I love you, and where I am from, when a man is in love he cannot hold back. I don't want to force you, but I believe you will see what I am made of in time."

There was a moment of silence. When her hand went to her chin and she said, as if thinking out loud, "I am one of the Han people, who you have just defeated in battle. How could you expect me to go off with my enemy?"

"Ha-ha." He burst out laughing at this statement. "What's the difference between the people of the Han dynasty and us Huns? Aren't we all human beings, who see with our eyes, hear with our ears, smell with our noses, and touch with our hands? Don't we share the same ambition, to enlarge our territory and enrich our people? I know where your prejudices come from! You Han considered yourself superior to other people. Remember, your government was weak and is now in chaos. Yes, we took the opportunity to invade to your territory, but we can run it better than your squabbling and weak emperor. You must remember, it was not us Huns that invaded out of aggression. Your government first invaded us; we invaded to protect our own. This is just the way of the world. Every king wants his citizens to have protection from murdering armies, so we needed to enlarge our territory. Only when we are strong enough will we feel safe. War is inevitable between two foreign tribes, willingly or otherwise. Only war can bring us peace!"

He fell silent until he said with all the sincerity he could muster, "What I mean is not just to offer you protection, but also to ask you to marry me. If you are against my proposal, I will grant you your freedom. I will not stop you from leaving."

Wenji listened to Tso-hyun carefully, secretly acknowledging that he had a point. He was right in that the emperor of the Eastern Han dynasty was weak and foolish. But should she accept her enemy's marriage proposal? She quietly considered the pros and cons. On the one hand, she wanted to be a virtuous woman. Her mother died of a broken heart because Wenji had transgressed society's ethics; on the other hand, she wanted to survive and, to be honest, she was infatuated with this spirited and handsome man. It seemed the only possible way to stay alive was to marry Tso-hyun. Sensing that she had made her decision, he offered her his hands. She had no choice but to take them. She would become the wife of Tso-hyun.

"Wonderful!" he said, calling in the servant and speaking to him in private. Soon a female servant arrived and took Wenji to another yurt to clean her up and get her changed. When she was led back to Tso-hyun's yurt, several dignitaries and other high ranking military men were stood around waiting. Tso-hyun had changed out of his military uniform into more regal garments. He held out his hand to her, and she realised the wedding ceremony was to happen immediately.

It was a simple but luxurious wedding. The soldiers celebrated the couple's health with many glasses of spirits. Milk tea was splashed outside, in accordance with a Hun ceremony. The soldiers sung and danced for the newly wedded couple. Wenji was given a luxurious fur gown to wear that followed the Hun tradition. Her shy smile and face warmed all in the tent. Out of warfare a gem was unearthed. Even the troops lit fireworks and celebrated with good will. It seemed that they were fond of their leader. Under the starry night, the couple swore to each other that they would be husband and wife. They held hands and danced round the fire the troops had lit.

Wenji was mesmerised by the events of the last few hours, but for the first time in months she felt relieved.

The next day she woke up to find her new husband missing. Then she remembered he had told her that the troops under his command were packing up for the move north.

She got up, got dressed, packed her meagre belongings and lovingly stroked her Guqin. She knew she was about to leave her homeland, and it was possible that she would never return. With these thoughts troubling her mind, she sighed and felt slightly sad. But she quickly pulled herself together. She was determined to pursue her new life.

ㄱ ㄱ ㄱ ㄱ ㄱ

In order to get to their northern homeland, the troops had to cross China's vast territory. Because the army was large and had to carry all their equipment, they made slow progress. Each day the yurts were set up and packed up. Wenji watched through the open curtain of her carriage and saw how the landscape gradually changed. She had plenty of time to reflect. The thought of marrying the enemy commander Tso-hyun played on her conscious.

She asked for a bamboo brush from her servant, and wrote down the turbulent feelings in her mind. A poem emerged as she wrote of her sorrows:

I sighed for my misfortune, born in troubled times
left by all I loved, one by one
alone, barely surviving
now to follow a new man. A Hun commander across
the gates of the northern frontier.
The journey; dangerous, long, tiresome.
A thousand valleys, mountains, rivers, far.
I can only look forward, no looking back.
My misfortunes have passed, but travel with me.
At night, sleep is hard to find.
My food, I eat out of nourishment,

my tongue not knowing the taste.

Tears moisten my eyes, never dry!

I am shameful of my weakness,

unable to commit suicide

or act as a virtuous woman.

*For these thousands of thoughts and
sorrows of my mind,*

I have no face to meet my fellow people.....

키 키 키 키 키

The further north they went, the icier the landscape became. It took almost half a year to reach their destination. Autumn became winter, with snow fakes drifting down from the sky. One morning upon arising, she looked outside. It was snowing heavily, and deep snow covered the ground. All was white. The landscape looked wild and barren, with not a human or animal to be seen. It seemed so lonely. Winter would be harsh living in the Northern Frontier. She was both amazed and frustrated by the wild land that was not fit for human beings to live in, not to mention growing crops and vegetables.

It was not until the early spring, when the snow started to melt, that people began to feel a sense of relief, of rebirth. Summer was lovely, as the grass waved in the wind as if a dancing, green sea. Life resumed. Animals emerged to drink from the ponds in the grassland. Such wildness made her happy. Summer though, was short lived, and too soon they were gripped by the cold of another long winter.

키 키 키 키 키

One day, when the sky seemed unable to empty itself of snow, Tsohyun fetched Wenji a thick fur coat and a pair of heavy snow boots. He tried to please her and help her through the cold winter.

In the beginning, she was uneasy about the customs and traditions of the Hun people. They ate more meat than vegetables, and spent a lot of time with their horses, holding different competitions. Children could ride a horse often before they could walk. She herself learned how to ride a horse with Tso-hyun's help. They entertained themselves by whistling tunes together. Yet they did not spend much time reading or writing. She enjoyed the differences, and embraced the new culture. By doing so, she quickly won the respect of Tso-hyun, the soldiers, and the common people. Wenji was clever enough to know that by immersing herself in their culture they would appreciate her more. She quickly learned to roast mutton on an open fire, which she shared with her husband. She ate with her fingers, and forced herself to laugh loudly and generously at witty humour. When the entertainers played the reed pipe, Wenji gazed at the musical instrument curiously, and felt the urge to learn to play it. She gazed at the wild grasslands as the music hung in the air. Sometimes though, when she was alone, she missed her past life and her parents, feeling a deep connection to her homeland. Her past life in the Han dynasty seemed like a remote dream.

Here, in the north, life was much simpler. As long as she was appreciated by the Tso-hyun she would have no cause for concern. With her beauty and gentility, she was regarded by the common people as the 'Goddess of the Grassland'.

Occasionally, when she reminisced about the past, her lost youth in the Han dynasty, she was overcome with emotion and would open her copy of the *Song of Poetry* and read poems until late at night. The book that she carried to this far land was now worn with use. One time, whilst reading, Tso-Hyun entered the tent. He was surprised to see Wenji writing.

"What are you writing? Ah, I forgot that your father was a famous scholar and that you are an educated woman yourself. No wonder... I saw how different you were from other women when

I first laid eyes on you. It is a saying among the Han gentry that knowledge changes and nourishes one's outlook".

Wenji closed the book and smiled, "My dear Hyun, you are only half right... life and experience change a person".

Tso-hyun nodded. Although he tried to mask it, he was nervous, because in truth, Wenji was forced to marry him. He secretly wondered if she was really happy, especially after what happened to her family and husband.

"Well," Wenji paused for a while purposely, "it's difficult to say." Seeing that he was concerned, she decided to tease him, "In the beginning I was uncomfortable, but as time has passed, I have grown to appreciate this harsh climate and your rough people."

"And me?"

"Of course you are the roughest... I love you", she said and smiled.

"When I met you, I saw you were carrying a musical instrument. What is that?"

"It's my Guqin." Wenji felt a lump in her throat. She felt a familiar longing for a soul mate, someone who understood her, like her last husband did.

"Will you play it for me? I have never heard the Guqin before."

Wenji was pleased he asked and said, "I learned to play the Guqin when I was six years old. I often play when I'm feeling troubled. Because of all the troubles I've endured, I have played for a long time. Then when I came here I had too many things on my mind. But now, after having been here enjoying while and beginning to appreciate the harsh beauty of the landscape, I have a renewed inspiration. I have composed a song for your people, the Hun tribes, to be played on the reed pipe."

"You can compose songs?" Tso-hyun was elated, "Every day you surprise me." He said cheerfully.

Wenji remarked, "Many feel that the Guqin is only fit for playing highbrow music to the elite, and usually it is only played by men. So it would be easier if I played a Hun song with a local musical instrument."

Wenji took out her reed pipe and gave a few tentative, warm-up blows. She smiled at him and started to play. Tso-hyun listened attentively, almost holding his breath. The music touched him, and stirred something deep in his heart. The melancholy tone thickened the air, and he sensed his wife's emotions. He looked at her face and the saw pain in her eyes. They held memories of death, war, starvation and humiliation.

When she finished he took her hands and asked, "What's the meaning of this song? Why does it make me feel so melancholy?"

Wenji smiled, "I will sing it for you. But this time I will play the Guqin at the same time." She began to sing:

When I was born, I was innocent.
As a young child our Han dynasty declined.
It was unkind to be born in these troubled times.
The world offered no warmth, only misfortune, one after another.
War everywhere. Death. Danger, not only mine.
The Hun invaded Han! Homeless.
Too much death, bodies everywhere.
I wanted to die as a virtuous woman, but I lacked the courage for suicide.
To survive, shamelessly, I married the enemy.
The traditions of the Hun and Han were different, so different.

Now, I tell of life with the music of the Guqin and a
reed pipe.
I will sing 'The Eighteen Songs of a Nomad Flute', to
tell you about my life.......

"Amazing." Tso-hyun looked at his wife with renewed respect. "Your playing allows me to feel your pain. By feeling your pain I know where mine is."

Wenji's faint smile reflected her acknowledgement of her music and her past. They left the yurt and sat under a million shining stars, so low she felt as if she could almost pluck them from the indigo sky. The couple sat together, shoulder to shoulder, silenced by the beauty.

"Have you finished composing all the pieces?"

"No, I have only completed five of the *Eighteen Songs of a Nomad Flute*."

"I wish you could sing to me forever," he said in a languid manner.

ㅋ ㅋ ㅋ ㅋ ㅋ

Two years later, Wenji gave birth to her first son. The following year, a second son was born. Wenji's position was greatly respected as she had given birth to two sons for a noble of the Hun dynasty. She was honoured as the Commander's wife.

ㅋ ㅋ ㅋ ㅋ ㅋ

Ten years passed. Although Wenji was happy, she always felt as if there was something missing. She missed the sweet scent of the flowers of her homeland. Flowers were not prolific in the north, not even in the spring.

Chapter Four

Cai Wenji returns to the Han dynasty

Fate, being what it is, is unpredictable. You never know what is to happen in the future. Misfortune could turn into fortune, and fortune into misfortune. Perhaps this was destiny playing a game, but people always tried to bend fate in their favour. An intelligent woman like Cai Wenji would also try and shape her own fate. She would follow her instincts and struggle to manage in troubled times as best she could.

Back in the Han dynasty, the warlords had almost done competing for the emperor's throne. The dynasty was divided into three, and became known as the Three Kingdoms (220-280 AD). Cao Cao, one of the greatest warlords in the Three Kingdoms, had united the northern part of the former Han dynasty, and had devoted himself to making a prosperous kingdom for himself and his subjects. He set up a system of governance that encouraged citizens to sew their fields without fear of punishment from harsh laws. He wanted a united China, and knew that to accomplish that task he must first have a firm foundation from which to do this.

Cao Cao had proclaimed himself King of the North. His army was strong, brave and disciplined. His only weakness was that he lacked a navy.

On the eastern border of his kingdom laid the vast sea. Once, when visiting the sea shore, the huge waves made him feel as if a tiny dust mite, and he could not help but write a poem to express his feelings:

> East of Jieshi mountain, I gaze at the blue sea.
> The water dances so gently, the mountain island
> towers above.
> Trees here grow thick, the grassy plains are lush.
> The autumn wind rustles in the air,
> great waves rise up.
> The path of the sun and moon, seems to rise up
> from the deep.
> The splendid Milky Way, seems to sink down below.
> Oh, I am so lucky, to be singing my song!

"Bravo." A clerk clapped his hands when he heard Cao Cao recite his grand poem. "My lord, you have a mind as expansive as a valley".

Cao Cao smiled, "It is this massive sea that arouses my awe of life." He could feel the destructive power of the sea from the headland on which he stood. The sea was so changeable, sometimes as still as a mirror, sometimes raging with the power to destroy. Suddenly, something his past master, Cai Han, taught him came to mind. "The water can sometimes bear the boat, but at the same time it can swallow it." Everything, including fame, reputation, success, and failure can be wiped out, like a cold stone lying at the bottom of the seabed.

"Alas!" Cao Cao sighed, hope lighting up his eyes. "I will unite the Three Kingdoms. No one is immortal, but my name will be known."

Thinking of Cai Han, Cao Cao's mind wandered to his daughter, Cai Wenji. She had a great reputation for her extraordinary beauty and talent. Such a woman was rare. He had heard that she had been captured by the Hun. Cao Cao wanted to get her back, as she was a magnificent woman with farsighted vision, easily outsmarting most men. She would be an asset to the dynasty. It would be a pity to abandon her to those barbarians. He remembered the child when he visited his master to discuss matters. There was one visitation when music drifted from the adjoining room. Cao Cao's heart was deeply touched. "Who's playing this beautiful music?" Cai Han laughed proudly, "Aha, my little daughter."

Cao Cao, with a pretended nonchalance asked, "How old is she?"

"She's only ten."

Cao Cao was astonished that a ten year-old girl could be so talented! At that moment, Wenji emerged from her room into the study to find her father and Cao Cao sitting and chatting together. She looked at Cao Cao with curiosity.

Cai Han introduced Cao Cao to Cai Wenji with much pleasure. "This is Cao Cao, my student."

"Uncle Cao Cao, it is nice to meet you." Cai Wenji said sweetly.

Cao Cao was enthralled by the vivacious confidence of this young girl. He said to himself that he must keep an eye on her, as soon she will be ripe.

He waited and watched, waiting for the right time to propose marriage to Cai Han. However, when the war broke out, he found himself too busy to consider such things. Now, despite his numerous wives, he found there was still a lingering emptiness. None of his concubines could fathom the depths of his mind. Perhaps Cai Wenji would be the exception.

Cao Cao could not forget the vivacious girl he had met all those years ago. Men treated their wives as decoration, like clothes or jewels, which could be abandoned and changed at whim. This metaphor, though, could only be fit for a common woman. When speaking of a talented woman such as Cai Wenji, however, it was a different story.

The sea aroused uneasiness in Cao Cao's mind. He asked his aide, "Do you remember Cai Han?"

His aide said knowingly, "Yes, of course. I heard after his death that his daughter was captured by the invading Huns. There has been no news of her since then." He was a reliable aide, and after having served his master for many years he could read his mind with ease. *Oh,* he thought, *Cao Cao has a plan. He wants to snatch Cai Wenji from the dragon's den and take her for himself.*

Not long after, Cao Cao united the northern part of the Han territory, and the King of the Huns arrived to congratulate him and offer tribute. Cao Cao received the Hun King with a large banquet, and treated him with the greatest respect. Their friendship deepened as they drank and feasted together.

The King of the Huns raised his cup and said, "Congratulations! I hope you can unite the Han dynasty soon, and we can begin trade between our two nations." He then shouted "*Ganbei!*" calling for all to raise their glasses and drain their cups.

Cao Cao raised his cup, "To friendship between our countries, *Ganbei!*" Then he made a motion calling for the entertainment must start, and the singers and dancers appeared. With blurry and shining eyes, the Hun King was greatly amused by the beauty and extraordinary talent of the women of the central plains of China. He was so excited and enthusiastic that he rose from his seat, and emulated the dancing girls.

Cao Cao, equally blurry-eyed asked, "You like the girls? Select the one you want as your entertainment."

"You are too generous."

Cao Cao hesitated, but the alcohol had given him courage, so he asked, "Ha, I'm seeking information of a woman who was said to be captured by your people twelve years ago. Her name is Cai Wenji... Have you heard of her?" He then turned to carefully study the face of the Hun King.

The king may have been drunk, but he was still wise enough to understand the implication of this question. "Yes, I know of her. She is the wife of Commander Tso-hyun."

Hearing this, Cao Cao restrained his emotions and kept the drunken smile on his face, "I think she should be with her people. Her father was once one of our most respected scholars and we owe a lot to him".

The Hun king hesitated, "She is greatly adored by Tso-hyun." Seeing Cao Cao's changed complexion, he quickly considered. He wanted an alliance, and there would be no good to come from irritating Cao Cao. The interests of his kingdom were far more important than a woman. Currently the Hun kingdom was suffering from a long drought. Food was scarce, and he needed money to support the people. Sensing an opportunity, the king laughed, "What a woman! She is not only the wife of Tso-hyun, but the people also love her. She is of great value to his region. Indeed she is of great value in general. But, if you want her back, I am sure we can come to some arrangement... I will try to persuade Tso-hyun to send Cai Wenji back to you." He then raised his drink once again, "*Ganbei*!"

"*Ganbei*!" Cao Cao smiled as he raised his cup.

力 力 力 力 力

"No! What? You want me to give up my wife and send her back to the Han kingdom? You are making a deal with a dangerous man. He is not to be trusted – he is not our friend!"

"He is the king of the Wei Kingdom. He rules over a vast proportion of the previous Han dynasty. We dare not offend him; he is much more powerful than we are. Moreover, we are neighbours. You can't start a war with your strong neighbour just for the sake of a woman."

"But you pay tribute to him?" Tso-hyun said with a sarcastic smile. Anguish overwhelmed him.

"Cai Wenji is not only your wife. She was a prize, a part of the spoils of war, so we will sell her back."

To part with his most beloved wife would be like a knife piercing his heart. However, he knew the king was right, that to fight with the Kingdom of Wei just for the sake of a woman was stupid. He also had to agree with the king that the Hun Kingdom was in desperate need of money to save the people from famine.

Tso-hyun spent many sleepless nights tossing and turning. Suddenly, he remembered how Wenji expressed her homesickness in her music. He then felt that it was enough for him to have been with her during her best years. They were worthy memories to be cherished. In this way, he made up his mind to part with his wife.

크 크 크 크 크

Wenji's maid had already told her about the deal. Cao Cao had sent an ambassador to bring her home. On hearing the news, Wenji's heart pounded. Never in her wildest dreams did she think that she would ever have a chance to see her birth place again. She could already smell the fresh spring air of her hometown. She would be free at last, no longer so isolated. After all her years living in the north as Tso-hyun's wife, she had grown accustomed to the local culture, but she had never forgotten who she truly was! She still longed for the place where she grew up. Yes, she belonged to Han dynasty, mentally and physically, no matter where she went or who she married. She longed to be with literate people. She never expected to be so happy when the news came. For a moment, she felt as if birds were singing in her heart. *But to go back home after twelve years of living as a Hun!* She had changed so much, and was much older now! She was afraid that her homeland would not accept her and the people perhaps consider her a traitor. It could all backfire if she went back. And what of her two boys?

Twelve years in the Hun Kingdom! What a twist of fate. Overcome with emotion, she felt as if everything was tangled, as if a ball of string. To be honest, she loved and hated the Hun. She loved Tso-hyun, and her two children she had with him, but she was not a Hun, and never really belonged to Hun people. What was right? What was wrong? If only she could see the future and know what to do. Then she remembered the hospitality that the Hun people had offered her. They were outgoing and gave themselves to her wholeheartedly. They were not as complicated as Han people. But she had no choice; the decision had been made already. How was she to live without her children? Why did life always play such cruel jokes on her?

Suddenly, she was overcome with a wave of strength. She would go back to her people. She did not belong here.

Besides, at thirty-five, her beauty was fading, and having reached middle age she could not guarantee a long-lasting love from Tso-hyun. Men changed so easily, including warriors like Tso-hyun. He took her like a common slave, and now she had been sold like a common slave.

At this moment, Tso-hyun came into her Yurt. He guessed that she had been told. Wenji raised her head, and looked directly in his eyes.

"You have heard the news." Tso-hyun said in a melancholy voice.

"You will sell me like a common slave?"

His gaze fell to the floor and he said nothing.

"You have not the nerve to tell me directly?"

Not hiding her bitterness very well, she said, "When I played you fifteen songs from my *Eighteen Songs of a Nomad Flute*, you remember I said there were three songs left?"

"Yes."

"I will finish the last three songs before I leave. I will play them to you before I go."

Tso-hyun was gloomy. Wenji was excited and anxious at the same time, but she did not show this. In truth, she would miss lying in the arms of her beloved husband.

지 지 지 지 지

A week later, she played the briskly paced sixteenth song of the *Nomad Flute*, playing the Guqin and singing in a deeply anguished voice:

> *Who sees the gloomy sorrow in my heart?*
> *This yurt, my home for twelve years,*
> *the wife of a Hun commander.*
> *Time flashed, we two now mature.*
> *Twelve years in this isolated desert, never did I expect*
> *to return home.*
> *Heaven again plays with me; I have fallen in love and*
> *given birth to two children... now he sends me back.*
> *I should be glad, but I shed tears.*
> *A part of me is the desert.*
> *The sun and moon is with heart,*
> *rising and falling as usual.*
> *But why has fate been so unfair? Not allowing me to*

go back earlier, till I gave birth to two children.
Now to be torn from them. I have no choice
but to say goodbye.

She proceeded to sing the next two songs, which were full of sorrow, confusion, and bitterness.

Tso-hyun heard Wenji sing with even deeper emotions than in the past. If the creator had made such a jade-like woman, why did her make her suffer? Wenji's turbulent life made his heart ache. Even he himself could never bear such misfortune. A tear ran down his face and onto the floor. He said, "You can go with ease. I will take care of our children. They will be my heirs."

Tso-hyun left the yurt, saying as he went, "You can leave now. Your ambassador and guides are waiting for you outside".

Cai Wenji felt a lump in her throat and a spasm in her stomach. Tears flooded her eyes. She was about to enter the coach when her two sons appeared. They tried to enter the coach but were stopped by the servant. The two boys began hysterically calling out to her, "Mother! Mother!"

Cai Wenji had no strength, and wailed as she was pushed into the carriage. As the coach pulled away, she kept looking back until she could no longer see the yurts of the Hun people. As if to mock her, the sky was a cloudless, deep blue. But later on it turned orange, the dusk sky holding the endless stories of Hun history.

ㅋㅋㅋㅋㅋ

To pass the time on her long journey, Wenji wrote about her life in the Hun Kingdom to help her cope with the gnawing pain.

Chapter Five

Back to the Han dynasty

Wenji would never forget the day when she left Hun Kingdom, escorted by Cao Cao's ambassadors. How sad it was to say goodbye to her children! She felt pain whenever she thought of her children waving and calling "Mother!" as they faded into the distance. She would awake drenched in sweat. She cried inside.

After two marriages, Wenji's heart was dead. She had no interest in a new relationship. The very afternoon of her arrival she was summoned by Cao Cao, who was too anxious to wait another day to allow her to freshen up. When Wenji was presented to him, with dishevelled hair and a tired face, broken and sad, Cao Cao was shocked. This beaten lady had no resemblance to the images he had carried in his mind for all those years. Her beauty and spirit had been broken. As she stood there, she did not care how she looked, or what he thought of her. Cao Cao felt great pity for her, but silently sighed with disappointment and sympathy. It was obvious that he had suddenly lost interest in her. But in order to be a gentleman, he welcomed her warmly.

Wenji smiled demurely and said in a flat voice, "Thank you."

"I had you reclaimed out of gratitude to my master Cai Han."
Cao Cao laughed, as if he was so happy to meet a long-lost friend.
"Could you sing a song for me?"

She did not want to sing but felt she must accept his request.
She began to sing the first song of the *Eighteen Songs of a Nomad
Flute* that she had composed.

What an extraordinary woman! Cao Cao thought as he listened
to the music. After she finished, Cao Cao clapped his hands, "You
deserved better treatment as the daughter of Cai Han."

Wenji tried to smile but said nothing.

"Is this what you have experienced and witnessed for twelve
years during your time with the Hun?"

Wenji nodded her head, "But I have seen the world".

"If I propose to you another marriage, will you accept it? His
name is Dong Si. He is one of my favourite lieutenants."

Wenji gasped in horror at the thought. How can a cold heart
enter marriage? Did she have a choice? Reluctantly, and out of self-
preservation, she demurely nodded yes.

He smiled, "You, a talented and handsome woman, must be with
a talented young man. Dong Si is such a man. He is an ambitious
and capable, you will like him I am sure. He is not only as strong as
a Hun, but also a classical historical scholar and philosopher. You
will have a lot of common".

"Thank you," Cai Wenji said. It did not matter to her anymore.

刁 刁 刁 刁 刁

Though Dong Si had long heard of the beauty and reputation of the
legendary woman Cai Wenji, he still could not accept the fact that
she was ten years older than he. Dong Si was dissatisfied with this
marriage. He had not reached the age to value the real capabilities
of women. He wanted a sweet, pretty faced virgin.

When they were married, Dong Si treated her with cold respect, but never visited her room. He indulged in the pleasures of other women. This suited Wenji, as all she wanted was to be left alone in peace to read her books and play her music. Never again did she want to be a pawn in life's travails. She had her memories, her books, and her music. She wanted nothing more.

Sometimes, at night she heard muffled laughter coming from Dong Si's room, where he entertained one concubine or another. Wenji's mind did not stir. She smiled consciously. She knew Dong Si married her only for the sake of obeying the imperial edict of Cao Cao.

One night, when Wenji was playing the Guqin, the tender melody finally drew Dong Si's the attention. *Who is playing this music*, he wondered? His concubine frowned, annoyed. Still, he could not help but listen to the music. He followed each note carefully. What music was she playing? He had never heard such music before. It was novel, tragic and disturbing. He could feel Wenji expressing her sorrows and her wrath towards life. Gone was his desire for the concubine and he dismissed her.

The next day Dong Si purposely passed by Wenji's room to see what she was doing and found her reading a history book. She noticed him but pretended not to, and continued reading. Dong Si was about to say something but changed his mind and backed out. She heard his footsteps retreat but did not raise her head.

경 경 경 경 경

Winter came quickly, and soon the ground was white with snow. Cold wind blustered and cut like a knife. The branches were stripped of the leaves, bare and gloomy. Wenji remembered the snow of the Hun Kingdom and thought of her children. Nevertheless, she appreciated the house she was in and the fact that she was not out on the streets.

Usually, she took no interest in the household activities, but the racket that erupted that winter afternoon could not be ignored. The house was filled with chaos and shouting. Dong Si's favourite concubine was crying, servants were whispering to each other. Peering out, she saw some of Cao Cao's guards apprehending and binding Dong Si's hands.

"What have I done?" Dong Si protested, "What crime have I committed?"

"What crime you have committed? Do you not remember opposing the wise words of our Lord Cao Cao?

Wenji took in a sharp breath. She knew this would be enough to sentence Dong Si to death.

"Ah. Do as you must." Dong Si held out his arms heroically and allowed the escort to bind him. Once they had tied him up, they dragged him out of the house.

Having witnessed this scene, Wenji had the feeling that her current peaceful life was about to come to an end. She suddenly felt a pang in her heart and compassion for Dong Si.

After Dong Si was arrested, everyone in the household was worried about their own well-being. Some left to try and find employment elsewhere, others moped around in uncertainty.

It was at this moment that Wenji realised that she was the only one who could save Dong Si's life. An idea occurred to her.

To everyone's astonishment, she took off her boots and walked bare foot through snow and ice to Cao Cao's palace.

When the court messenger saw Cai Wenji standing in front of him without a coat and with bare feet, he was visibly shocked, "Madam Dong, why do you come here... like this?"

"I have come here to meet with Lord Cao."

"I will tell him." He looked at her bare feet and shook his head. He saw traces of blood on them.

"Would you like me to ask a servant to bring you a pair of boots?"

"No, thank you."

Cao Cao was in discussion with his advisers and assistants, when the messenger intruded. "My Lord, Madam Dong is here and asks to with meet you".

"What for?"

"I believe that she is here to beg for mercy for Dong Si."

"On what right does she ask a favour for him? Doesn't she know how Dong Si insulted me?"

"My Lord, you must know that she walked here without wearing boots, in bare feet. Her feet are frozen and bleeding from the ice".

Cao Cao was shocked and appalled when he heard the miserable state this famous lady was in. He quickly stood up and paced around the room. How could they allow such an important lady to suffer like this? "Bring her here."

Cao Cao was anxious, afraid to meet Wenji in this situation. He did not speak while he waited for her to enter.

To the anguish of all those in attendance, everyone could see Wenji's blue and bleeding feet when she walked in. When she stood in front of the group of men, they were all too baffled to speak. She looked at them, staring each of them in the face, finally settling her glare on Cao Cao. Her aura of calm determination made them all feel uncomfortable, reminding them of when they were children and their mother would shout at them for being naughty. Before the effect wore off, she kowtowed to Cao Cao and paid her respects to him. With head bowed she said in a respectful but persuasive voice, "My lord, you have sentenced Dong Si, my husband, to death because he offended you. As his wife, I humbly ask for you to withdraw your sentence."

"Why should I?" He asked. "Throughout history, sage emperors were ready and open to criticism. They did not sentence a loyal official to death just because he had another opinion. Consider the famous story of when the King of Qi was unwilling to hear the criticism of others, preferring only flattering words. That is until one day, Qi Xiu's adviser remonstrated to the King using a metaphor. He told the King of Qi of the conversation between him and his wife about who was the wisest man in the kingdom. The King of Qi was enlightened by the story, and announced a new law. All officials who pointed out his mistakes directly to his face would receive good reward. If they wrote to remonstrate with him, they would receive a modest reward…" She continued, "What do you think my father would have advised you on this matter? Do you really want to sentence Dong Si to death just because his opinion was different from yours, even though he would defend you and your kingdom with his life?" Once she had finished, she stood quietly in front of him.

Cao Cao was deeply moved by her bravery and sincerity. She truly was the daughter of his mentor. Alas, he wondered why that stupid Dong Si could not cherish such an excellent wife.

His first words were, "Servant, bring medication for Madam Dong's feet, and bring her some socks and boots." This was not what she wanted to hear, so she continued to stand and wait quietly.

His voice squeaked a bit when he made his pronouncement, "I have already announced his death sentence."

Cai Wenji persisted in a low but calm voice that all could hear, "My lord, you have many horses of good breeding. Why don't you ask someone to announce your mercy by riding such a horse?"

For a full minute he pondered. He was fully convinced that the woman in front of him was the same as the girl in his memory. He said in a low voice, "I am impressed by Madam Dong's virtue and bravery. I grant her request. Free Dong Si. Do it now!"

"Thank you, Sage." Cai Wenji said as she kowtowed to Cao Cao once again. Being told to stand up and go with the servants, she retreated from the court and with the greatest dignity.

Everyone in the court was filled with admiration for Madam Cai Wenji. Cao Cao said after her, "I wish you happiness in your latter life, and no more suffering. You deserve happiness."

ㄱ ㄱ ㄱ ㄱ ㄱ

When she was walking to the carriage that had been bought for her, Wenji felt the pain in her feet. Each step was like a knife. Yet, when she had hurried to the palace earlier, there was no thought of pain.

Chapter Six

Dong Si

Dong Si was prepared to die a martyr, when suddenly a guard rushed in with a messenger. The messenger announced, "Because of the virtue and fidelity of Madam Cai Wenji, I grant you freedom. But you will not escape punishment. You will be deprived of the position of lieutenant, but your income will remain, by order of Cao Cao".

Dong Si's mind was slow to grasp what he was hearing. Confused, he was supported out of the cell whilst the messenger described the entire event, and how his wife risked her life for his. He was free. Only once he was on the street did he realise that he was safe. He took a breath of fresh air, and saw the colourful world as if for the first time. At the same time, he felt guilt, as the one who saved him was his neglected wife. It would be different now.

He rode the horse Cao Cao had provided him as if riding with the wind. He wanted to get back home urgently. When he arrived he found some of his staff and relatives gone, and others about to leave. He ignored them as if they did not exist, and instead hurried towards Wenji's room. Bursting in, he saw a servant carefully attending her wounded feet. Seeing them, he felt a pain in his heart as they were as swollen as the feet of a fat pig.

Dong Si went over to Wenji, held her feet in his trembling hands and blew warm breath on her frozen feet. He told the servant to leave, and he himself attended to her. He thought about his folly, how could he have neglected this incredible woman. Tears welled up in the corners of his eyes.

飞 飞 飞 飞 飞

Months later, when the blossoms of spring were in bloom, Dong Si sat reading a book with Cai Wenji, and there was laughter and affection between the couple.

Dong Si stood, and held out his hand, "Yes?" she asked.

"Let's wander around and enjoy the peach flowers." She took his hand and smiled to him as she stood up.

That afternoon, as they sipped wine under the warm spring sun, Dong Si asked, "Do you play chess?"

"Of course... my father taught me." As the board and pieces were being bought to them, he asked, with a touch of concern, "Do you prefer the Northern Frontier to living here?"

"Ha." Wenji smiled and caught a falling peach flower petal. She stared at it, her mind elsewhere. Then she said, "I created a series of songs about the desert. I called these songs the *Eighteen Songs of a Nomad Flute*. Would you like to hear them later?"

"Yes." He guessed it was the tragic music that he heard that night before he was arrested.

Later, before retiring, they went to the study, and Wenji took out her beloved Guqin and sang some of the songs she had composed.

Like all who heard her music, Dong Si was deeply touched. At this moment, he understood who Wenji really was and how she could embody such emotion in music. Her life, her experiences, and her suffering were as vivid as a picture. He asked, "Would you mind if I amend your music a bit to make it more suitable for a Han audience?"

Cai smiled brightly with happiness at hearing these words. Her thoughts meandered far away. She thought of her two boys and hoped they were healthy. After years of waiting, struggling, and suffering, she had finally regained the happiness and security she had felt as a child. Her new life radiated with light and warmth like the spring outdoors. It seemed that life was fair after all but full of surprises. Perhaps there was power in Cao Cao's wish for her?

Thereafter, Dong Si and Wenji devoted a great deal of time to modifying the *Eighteen Songs of a Nomad Flute* so that they were a better cultural fit for Han audiences. After years of hard work, Dong Si was able to play the music in the court many times, and gradually the music spread from the elite class down to the civilians. Till this day, the Chinese people love this music, and it is part of their national identity.

People remember that this music was made by a legendary woman, a musical genius, the daughter of the renowned scholar Cai Han.

Bibliography

Cai Wenji (184 AD-239 AD): created *The Eighteen Songs of a Nomad Flute.* (Chinese: 胡笳十八拍; pinyin: Hújiā Shíbā Pāi).

Cai Han (133AD-192AD): A great scholar and father of Cai Wenji. He composed many long enduring pieces of prose. As a politician, he was devoted to the citizens, and it was for this reason that he often challenged the emperor.

King Tso-hyun: In the story, I referred to him as Tso-hyun, but his correct name is King Tso-hyun. I did this to remove confusion, and to distinguish him from the King of the Hun.

It is unclear when King Tso-hyun was born or died. He was a great nobleman in the Hun tribe and lived in the east part of the Hun territory.

Cai Wenji was captured by King Tso-hyun, and was married to him for twelve years, bearing him two sons. Later, in order to form an alliance with the Han, and Cao Cao, King Tso-hyun sent Cai Wenji back to Han China.

Dong Zhuo (?-192 AD): It is unclear when Dong Zhuo was born. He was one of the warlords at the end of Eastern Han dynasty. He was born in Longxi (modern-day Gansu province). At the end of Han dynasty, he was appointed as governor of the Bing region. He had the emperor under his control, as well as the emperor's vassals. Under his rule, the Han dynasty ceased to exist except in name.

At the end of Han dynasty, Dong Zhuo was successful in the war with Qiang tribe, and suppressed the rebellions of Huang Jing and Liang Zhou. He saved the emperor to only then used him to make royal decrees, as he himself had no royal blood.

Dong Zhuo invited Cai Han back to his office in the capital. In the year 190, Dong Zhuo was defeated in the war with another warlord

Yuan Shao. He retreated into Chang'an. However, because of his cruelty, he was killed by his own men, who were encouraged to do so by Wang Yun, another powerful official in the Han dynasty.

Cao Cao (155 AD-220 AD): the king of Wei during the Three Kingdoms period. He was a politician, strategist, and poet. At the end of Han dynasty, Cao Cao went on a punitive expedition towards the four areas under the authority of the emperor. He not only succeeded in exterminating the rebellion troops inside the Han dynasty, but also the foreign tribes, such as the Hun and the, Xianbei. He united the territory of northern China. In the year 213 AD he established the Wei Kingdom.

Cao Cao had developed his talent in literature and military strategy since he was a young man. His father was once the prime minister of the Han dynasty. Cao Cao studied under Cai Han, Cai Wenji's father. When Cao Cao died, his son Cao Pi succeeded him as the king of Wei.

Wei Zhongdao: Cai Wenji's first husband. As noted in the story, he died at a young age. He was born to a noble family in Hedong city. The Wei family had a great reputation during the Han dynasty.

Dong Si: a lieutenant in Cao Cao's army and Cai Wenji's last husband. Cai Wenji saved Dong Si's life as reflected in the story.

References:

Books:

1. *The Legend of a Strong Girl* from *Book of the Later Han* by Fan Ye (398-445)

2. *Biographies of Dong Zhuo,* in the *Fan Book* by Li Xian (dates unknown)

3. Records of the *Three Kingdoms* by Chen Shou (233-297)

4. *The Book of Wei*, by Wang Shen. (Unknown date)

Academic papers:

1. Xing Xiuling, *The talented woman in the troubled time* – Cai Wenji, 05, 2015, China Academic Journal Electronic publishing House.

2. Wang Ai Jun, *Cai Wenji, the one who was saved by Cao Cao,* China Academic Journal Electronic publishing House.

3. Yan Yuan, *the tragic songs of Nomad Flute,* China Academic Journal Electronic publishing House.

4. Shao Congming, *The tragic life of Cai Wenji,* Yan Bian University.

Internet sources:

Eighteen Songs of a Nomad Flute, https://so.gushiwen.org/shiwenv_9976b9da5244.aspx

Dong Zhuo, https://baike.baidu.com/item/董卓/17359?fr=aladdin

Cao Cao, https://www.gushiwen.org/Author_b8db2d30a1.aspx

Wei Zhongdao, https://baike.baidu.com/item/卫仲道/4623672

Dong Si, https://baike.baidu.com/item/董祀/110374

Zuo Xianwang, https://baike.baidu.com/item/左贤王/1164749

Cai Wenji, http://hx5q.com/detail/au_2661.whtml

Story TWO

Shangguan Wan'er

Shangguan Wan'er

This Chinese figure painting in China shows Shangguan Wan'er reflecting on her decision to serve for the empress Wu Zetian.

Chapter One

The early years of Shangguan Wan'er

The Tang dynasty (618-907 AD) was one of the most prosperous dynasties of ancient China. During this dynasty, our legendary woman, Shangguan Wan'er, was famous not only for her literature, but also because she became a prime minister. She was blessed with good political instincts and farsightedness, and manoeuvred between the different political powers successfully. Luckily or unluckily, she had been involved in politics since she was a child, and was frequently a victim of politics throughout her life. At one stage, Shangguan Wan'er had so much power that it seemed to many that she was able to summon the wind and the rain at will. However, in the end, she lost the political game because of her compassionate nature. The fact that she was a woman, though, meant that her fate had already been sealed long before her downfall.

Early in the Tang dynasty, the third emperor, Li Zhi (Tang Gaozong, 628-683) had married a beautiful woman named Wu Zetian. Li Zhi was a witty and ambitious emperor, diligent in public affairs, and well-liked by the people. Historians called his rule the 'legacy of the era of good government of Zhenguan', a reference to the successful rule of his father, emperor Taizong. Through his continuous endeavours the dynasty strengthened its central power and expanded its territory. During his rule, the Tang dynasty reached the peak of its prosperity during what was arguably the most expansive period of ancient China. The small neighbouring states paid tribute to the emperor. Because of the openness of the dynasty, it attracted many scholars and foreigners from all over the world. Chang'an, now located in modern-day Zhejiang province, was considered a global capital at the time.

Within the nobility, political struggles were intense. In order to balance the power of two different factions, and weaken the power of some important officials, emperor Tang Gaozong decided to govern the dynasty together with his wife Wu Zetian. He respected Wu Zetian's suggestions, and the couple cooperated well and strengthened their control over the central government. Wu Zetian learned how to deal with public affairs. When Tang Gaozong was dying, he fully entrusted Wu Zetian to read and act upon official documents. She did, but she needed up manipulating the political situation accordingly to her desire. At first, she issued instructions from behind the scenes. As time passed, Wu Zetian pushed herself onto the historical stage and into the political spotlight.

Shangguan Yi, the prime minister, remonstrated with Emperor Tang Gaozong many times, warning him to be careful of Wu Zetian, as her ambitions had grown too expansive. Gradually, Wu Zetian formed a secret clique to help her gain complete control of all political affairs. She had tasted the sweetness of being at the top and craved the adulation of the people.

Emperor Tang Gaozong's health diminished day by day. There were many rumours about Wu Zetian; that she disrupted the court discipline and had been changing the ethics of court. Emperor Tang Gaozong and Wu Zetian had one son, Prince Li Xian, who was seventeen years-old when Tang Gaozong made the last imperial edict. He was a handsome young man, but was physically frail, and often bed-ridden. In his early days he showed little interest in royal duties, but as he got older he became more interested as he realised that he had the ability to control. Civilians gossiped and speculated about who would be the next emperor after Tang Gaozong. Most people thought that Wu Zetian would retain control, yet they still doubted whether a female was capable of ruling the dynasty.

Prime minister Shangguan Yi pleaded with the emperor, "My lord, I don't think it is wise to choose Wu Zetian as the empress to support the crown prince. Rather, you should pass power directly to the crown prince."

"Why? Can't you see Wu Zetian has the potential to govern the court well? Has she not been successful in helping me? For many years, we achieved remarkable success in governing the kingdom together. Is it not sensible for her to continue and support my son?"

"It's wrong!" refuted Shangguan Yi, "Traditionally, women have not participated in politics, and under her court discipline will erode. Do you think Wu Zetian will be content only to help the prince? Has it not occurred to you that she wants to be the empress herself? If she succeeds, who will be her successor? The royal bloodline will not continue."

Tang Gaozong felt his headache. He was tired and wanted to rest. He was aware that much of the court was under Wu Zetian's control, but if he did not pass the throne to her, there would be a raging storm. Wu Zetian already had the control she needed to remain in power.

Shangguan Yi did not give up and continued, "No, my lord. Please think twice before you make up your mind. If you change the ruling of the court and the tradition of our ancestors, the entire kingdom will blame you. Our dynasty, which our ancestors fought hard to build, will be ruined by her hands. Throughout history, women were not allowed such power. I don't think you need me to explain the reason, but I will. Firstly, compared to men, women are usually too emotional and sensitive. Those who are not are either whores or serpents. It is their duty to take care of the family. Yes, of course in history there have been cases when the emperor's mother has helped their son rule the country by offering useful suggestions. But such a woman was just supporting the emperor, not ruling herself. I believe Wu Zetian has the ambition to rule the kingdom herself. Moreover, Wu Zetian will use any means to pursue power. She has been calculating and determined, irrespective of the consequences".

Tang Gaozong sighed, and tried to reconsider, but he felt he had no choice but to pass the throne to Wu Zetian. Perplexed, Shangguan Yi's face became distorted and grew increasingly concerned. Shangguan Yi continued in an even more determined way. He exposed more truths about Wu Zetian to Tang Gaozong, greatly wounding the emperor's pride in the process. The emperor just wanted Shangguan Yi to leave him in peace. Tang Gaozong sank into deep meditation. Yes, he was right on some points. Of course, he heard rumours in the court. Did Wu Zetian really have her opponents killed to increase her power? Was she really so ambitious that she would try to become empress instead of just supporting their son? Even a vicious tiger does not eat its clubs. How could a woman do such things? Tang Gaozong found himself in an awkward position. Finally convinced, he decided to follow Shangguan Yi's advice, to make the requested changes in the imperial edict. However, his eyes were blurred, and his spirit brought low by this decision.

Indeed, as Tang Gaozong turned a blind eye to Wu Zetian, Wu Zetian was busy placing her many spies throughout the court. Every palace maid or eunuch could be an 'ear-to-the-wall' who reported to Wu Zetian. Soon, the conversation between Shangguan Yi and Tang Gaozong was reported back to her. Wu Zetian felt panicked. What if her husband followed Shangguan Yi's suggestion and changed his mind? So before the emperor made the changes to the imperial edict, she rushed into her husband's chamber, knelt down and burst out crying. This surprised Tang Gaozong not a bit.

"Did I do something wrong to make you angry at me?" Wu Zetian moaned.

"My dear, what makes you say that?"

"There are rumours about me. Some say that I plan to become empress myself. I hear the palace maids gossiping and whispering bad things about me. It would seem that there are many court officials who are prejudiced against me. All that I have done was for your sake, and the people's. It is you who asked me to investigate the rebellions in the court! Of course, by doing so I have upset many people, especially some members of the nobility, and now they want revenge. For twenty years I have devoted myself to the people. You know my dedication. I have no other intent. You should know me better than anyone else in the world."

All this was said with anguish, tears falling down her face, the back of her hand pressed against her forehead. Every so often, for effect, she would sniff or wipe her runny nose with a silk handkerchief.

Tang Gaozong was embarrassed and saddened. He gently wiped the tears from Wu Zetian's face and helped her up. He said, "I am not an old fool yet. I can judge right from wrong." He waved a hand to instruct a eunuch to lead Wu Zetian away. He was tired and weak, and needed to be alone.

Although she did not become the empress, her life was spared. The edict, in theory, said that she was to support the prince in governing the court. However, she already had the power, if not the name, of empress. She in turn would bide her time and manipulate the situation as best she could.

In 683, Wu Zetian ended the pretence of governing on behalf of the prince, and she announced to all and sundry that the prince was too weak and foolish to rule properly. In order to strengthen her power to take the throne for herself, she began to eliminate officials who opposed her influence. One by one, they fell by the wayside. She eliminated Zhangsun Wuji, the previous prime minister, and an esteemed scholar of the dynasty. Of course, she had Shangguan Yi, the very man who remonstrated with Emperor Tang Gaozong, in her sights. To be honest, Wu Zetian did feel pity for Shangguan Yi because he was a good official. But as he had opposed her, she would have to get rid of him. The time was not right, however, as she did not want to be seen as eliminating him for revenge. In time, she secretly bribed a high-ranking official to accuse Shangguan Yi of plotting a rebellion against the court. Shangguan Yi was placed in the jail to await his punishment – death.

Our heroine, Shangguan Wan'er, was the granddaughter of Shangguan Yi. According to the law of the time, all generations of a condemned person were to receive the same sentence. In this case, as one member of the family had plotted a rebellion, all his family members were also to be condemned to death. Luckily however, Shangguan Wan'er was still a baby at this time. Wu Zetian, in a moment of weakness or compassion felt sympathetic towards this baby, so she pardoned the mother and daughter, but with one harsh condition – that they remain in the palace as slaves. The mother, Ms Zheng, had no choice as she had to protect her child. Swallowing her pride, she agreed to the humiliating punishment.

Wu Zetian, with a faint and mischievous smile, had saved the mother and the daughter's life. But as if she secretly plotted to toy with them, as if she were playing a game of Go. She wondered if Shangguan Wan'er, growing up in the court, would have the ability to educate herself, and would seek revenge in the future. Would there be a bloody revenge? It was these games of intrigue that Wan'er would have to overcome. It was Wu Zetian, the cat, playing with Wan'er, the mouse.

So, the baby and her mother settled into the servant's quarters as court slaves. At this time in ancient China, slaves were the lowest social class. They had little freedom and could only marry other slaves. Ms Zheng, carefully protecting Wan'er, did her best to serve Wu Zetian and humbly lowered herself by saying "a thousand thanks." There was always an underlying threat of danger.

列 列 列 列 列

The years passed, and Wan'er grew up in the court as a slave. She did not know her past, as Ms Zheng was afraid that Wan'er would rebel or be sullen if she knew her family background – it was too dangerous. Besides attending court school, Wan'er was also educated by Ms Zheng herself. Wan'er was quick to learn. Nevertheless, growing up in the court, and being from nobility noble family, it would seem from the beginning Wan'er could never escape her fate of being involved in political life.

There was, however, one advantage of growing up in the court. The court had a well organised educational system, especially, when Wu Zetian was in charge, as she recognised the importance of education for all. Moreover, Wu Zetian no longer allowed the eunuchs to govern the scholarly studies, but rather appointed famous scholars to teach and oversee lessons. Lessons encompassed calligraphy, mathematics, history, philosophy, poetry, writing, and chess, and eventually the military examination was also added to the Imperial exam. Wu Zetian ordered all the people living in the court, including the court slaves, to attend school. This law was especially made for Wan'er, for Wu Zetian wanted to know the results of her gamble.

Wan'er was naturally endowed with unusual intelligence, and quickly distinguished herself among the students and officials of the court. Her mother was of course a great help in advancing her knowledge. Wan'er loved poetry and chess, and excelled at both. The masters were amazed at this young girl's quick intelligence.

One day, when Wan'er was fourteen years old, Wu Zetian inquired about the court school studies, and the master casually mentioned Shangguan Wan'er's name as a star pupil. This immediately gained Wu Zetian's attention. She suddenly decided that she wanted to meet the girl. She wanted to judge whether she was friend or foe.

As a slave, Wan'er experienced great hardship. Believing she was a slave, she knew how precarious their situation was. She worked hard, but soon learnt to observe the faces of the nobility for indications of discontent. As a slave, she felt like a fish out of water and was pleased that she was being educated. With education, she felt there was some hope for a better life, she was quick to learn and keen of intellect, unlike most slaves or servants, who paid little attention to education. What spare time she had she used to read every book she could get her hands on, irrespective of the topic. And, with her wonderful memory, she managed to retain all information. She loved history, as she believed it gave her a good grasp of many relevant things. Gradually, Wan'er formed her own impressions of court life.

Through her studies, Wan'er learnt a great deal about Empress Wu Zetian. She wondered if she, a lowly slave, could meet the Empress one day, or even just catch a glimpse of this powerful and beautiful woman. A feeling of awe crept into her mind at the thought. She was grateful for the education she had received, knowing it was the Empress who set such high standards.

Wan'er pursed her lips and innocently asked, "Mother, do you think that I would ever get to meet Empress Wu?"

Ms Zheng hesitated before replying, "I hope you never meet her."

"Why?" Wan'er was surprised by her mother's words.

"Because...there things you do not know."

"Like what?"

Her mother knew that Wan'er had reached the age and maturity to learn about her family's past.

"If I tell you, it could make you very unhappy. Promise me after hearing what I have to say you must not get angry, especially with the empress, nor should you lose your mind. This is your first practical lesson on self-control. You will need to think twice before you leap."

"You are worrying me Mother… I will, as always. But what is it?"

Ms Zheng told Wan'er about her family background, and that her grandfather and father who were killed by Wu Zetian for no crime other than wanting the best for the Tang dynasty.

Wan'er burst out crying, "It's not true. You're lying!"

"It's the truth." Ms Zheng said bitterly.

Wan'er sank into silence as tears fell down her face. But even so, she kept calm and thought while sobbing. Her mind ran every-which-way. It troubled her to think that Wu Zetian was her enemy. She had admired Wu Zetian, but this was too much.

After some half an hour of consideration she said in a voice of controlled-calm, "I will take every opportunity to get close to Empress Wu, and in time our revenge will come".

Her mother said with concern, "Don't, you must behave as if you are grateful to her. However wicked Wu Zetian is, she did save our lives!"

This was another thunderbolt for Wan'er to ponder, *why did Wu Zetian let my mother and I live? What game is she playing, and why did she choose to educate me? Was Wu Zetian not afraid that she, Shangguan Wan'er, would seek recompense? Was she so arrogant?*

It would seem the mouse was now ready to do her own playing with the cat!

Chapter Two

Shangguan Wan'er as a young adult

As mentioned earlier, news of Shangguan Wan'er brilliance came to the attention of Wu Zetian. Wu Zetian wanted to assess this young girl's intentions, to watch her closely. She learnt that she was not only clever, but showed signs that she would be a most beautiful woman. Intriguingly enough, the young girl showed no indication of resentment.

Wu Zetian was surprised; at fourteen, this girl was showing such talent! Indeed, she must be a rare treasure. The girl would probably be useful in the future. "Bring her to me in the morning. In fact, let there be a competition." Wu Zetian said to an assistant.

The news was delivered to Wan'er that she was to meet Wu Zetian the next day. After tossing and turning in bed, she had a sleepless night. Finally, she would meet this woman who dared to break the will of the emperor and the law, who killed her grandfather and father, and made her and her mother into slaves.

Upon arising, Wan'er chose her makeup and clothes with care. Using a brush, she applied a plum flower colour to her forehead. She wore a lemon-coloured upper garment, and high-waisted, white-coloured skirt, which revealed the top of her blooming bosom. She did not want to look too beautiful, modest perhaps was best. Her finished face made her look like a budding peony in early spring.

Having been brought to the interview, Wan'er waited for Wu Zetian. She was told to sit and wait near the table with the other females who had been told to come: students, wives of officials, and servants.

They were allowed to chat whilst they waited. Wan'er was social and enjoyed talking to them, and they liked Wan'er as she would talk to all, including the slaves. Despite understanding her level of intelligence and accumulated knowledge, she was not arrogant. Wan'er had long understood the importance of having friends of all levels if she was to survive in the court, which was full of tricksters and schemers. She needed 'ears'.

Looking at herself in the bronze mirror, she did know if she was more excited, nervous, or afraid to meet Empress Wu. Wan'er could not figure out what may be expected of her, but was conscious that this meeting could change her life.

Sometimes she wondered if she was born in a lucky time or a bad time. If Wu Zetian were not in power, the court school for female officials and lower class women would not exist. Seldom did any female dare to challenge the tradition of the court, as most people considered it unnatural and disastrous for a woman to have power in the court. This was what her grandfather believed, and that was another reason why Wu Zetian eliminated her father and grandfather and broke up her family. However, at the same time, Wu Zetian opened the way for Wan'er to be educated – she could have blocked her education – as if by giving her foe an education, she was creating a stronger adversary. Or perhaps by educating her, but keeping her as a slave, she knew that Wan'er would forever be disgruntled.

Being a female, she had lower class status. Men treated women as if they were items of clothing that could be discarded at a whim. Men could also have more privileges in court, where few women were allowed to enter. Women were expected to make themselves look attractive for men to ensure their survival. Few men of the time were known treat women with the respect of an equal, from beginning to the end, because they regarded women as inferior, without thoughts or feelings. Was this what Wu Zetian had decided for Wan'er? Yet, Wu Zetian encouraged woman to be educated, to compose poetry, and be literate. Wan'er's thoughts were interrupted, as a eunuch announced, "Empress Wu has arrived!"

All the females stood up and lowered their heads, whilst saying, "Long live my Empress."

"Sit down." Wu Zetian said with a radiant smile. Wan'er felt the aura of power emanating from Wu Zetian. She looked majestic and spoke with authority. The awe that Wan'er felt was admiration and fear. She was looking at a saint and a demon. Wan'er's instinct told her that Wu Zetian was covertly intrigued by her.

Wan'er kept her head lowered, avoiding Wu Zetian's eye contact, when Wu Zetian announced, "You are required to create a poem. This will be done here and now, with a time limit. I want to check how much good education is doing you. All of you have the potential to advance in the future, and poetry, as you should know, is a measure of a person's intelligence, skill, and knowledge. This test is important for your future. Do you understand?"

"Yes." They all answered with deep respect and concern.

Wu Zetian nodded for the eunuch to light the incense and issue a brush, ink and paper to each student, whilst saying, "You are free to write a poem about your life in the court. You must be finished before the incense burns out." Then she and the other high officials in attendance waited there for the young women to write their poems, speaking quietly amongst themselves as they waited.

Wan'er looked out of the window and sank deep into thought. The bamboo in the courtyard gently danced in the breeze. Shadows darkened pockets of the grounds. She could hear the flowing sound of the Luo River trickling happily along. Suddenly, she had an urge to embrace the beautiful scenery. It cheered her up. Enlightened, she lowered her head to her paper and began writing. In her mind, she pictured the scene when the dawn broke; the officials gathered in front of the court, waiting for the gate to open to conduct their business. It was a busy yet peaceful morning, when she was expected to ride the horse and be the messenger of the court. Her strokes with the bamboo bush flowed with ease, the ancient characters coming to life to tell her story.

Silently the Luo River flows to the east, far away.

Just before dawn, thick in autumn.

Silently, moonlight shines.

The magpie warbles to announce good news,

Cicadas chatter noisily amongst themselves.

Riding a horse, I follow the riverside,

With hundreds of court officials waiting.

Wan'er finished the poem, and looked at the incense to see that it was only half burnt.

Wu Zetian pounced on Wan'er's paper and quickly read the work. While Wan'er was writing the poem, Wu Zetian was surreptitiously appraising Wan'er – indeed, she will be a beauty. The young girl had proud and intelligent eyes, both alert and focused.

Wu Zetian, with a slight side smile, nodded her head with approval.

As the other poems were finished, Wu Zetian, read each in turn. Wu Zetian had asked for the most prodigious students to be bought to her, including Wan'er.

The officials had their turn to read the poems, and as they did there were smiles and nods of approval. Later, as they discussed the poems, they expressed that certainly Wan'er was extraordinary, with an expansive and thoughtful mind! Her poem was not full of the flowery words and phrases that were the trend in the dynasty at the moment. It was rather euphemistic and refreshing. And she had managed to get it done in only a few minutes, while her calligraphy was as advanced as any elder master. Most impressive. For now though, they said nothing to the gathering.

Impatiently, Wan'er waited to hear what Wu Zetian had to say. Wu Zetian offered a smile to all and said, "Thank you, you can all go… but not you Shangguan Wan'er."

After the others had gone, the empress again gave Wan'er a glowing smile. In fact, Wu Zetian saw something more than the officials had in her poem – Wan'er's ambition. Indeed, Wan'er was clever. Behind the words there was a code of sorts; the girl wrote as if she aspired to gain an imperial mandate. She used clean and fresh phrases, and in a few lines described the peaceful and prosperous nature of the Tang dynasty. The line *The magpie warbled to announce good news* was definitely written in praise of a prosperous time. While at the same time, *Cicadas chattered noisily*, hinted that there were still people unsatisfied with the government at the moment. Shangguan Wan'er was farsighted enough to see that whatever the circumstances were, the responsibility of the government to the people would never disappear. In these a few sentences, Wan'er's opportunism and political astuteness was revealed.

"How old are you?" Wu Zetian asked.

"Fourteen, Madam Empress."

"Aha, a fourteen-year-old girl with such intelligence and peerless talent. It is rare!" With curiosity, Wu Zetian asked, "You will be rewarded. What do you want?"

"Nothing for me my Empress. But... but...if I was given more books and time to read?"

"I will see that that happens. This is the best reward that could be asked for. From now on, you are allowed to further your studies using the historical books of the court. And you are to undertake a junior position in the Imperial court."

Wan'er kowtowed, "Thank you Your Highness!"

That evening, Wan'er could not help but feel confused. How could this paragon of corruption be at the same time so majestic in appearance and supportive of her talents? At that moment, her admiration towards Wu Zetian overwhelmed her hatred. What she found was a sage empress, rather than a hard woman, as rumours had painted her. Her intentions of revenge had all vanished. Maybe people were wrong in their opinion of Wu Zetian? But then her mother's story of death and betrayal returned vividly, and hatred crept throughout her body once more.

Shangguan Wan'er was uncertain in her new official role. On the one hand, she had a genuine concern about integrity within politics, just as her grandfather had. However, she was also troubled by her feelings towards Wu Zetian, who was her natural enemy, but who played the game of being Wan'er's benefactor.

When Wan'er told her mother about her promotion, Ms Zheng slapped Wan'er's face before Wan'er could finish speaking. Ms Zheng said angrily, "How dare you serve the enemy who had killed your father, my husband, and also your grandfather, who was my father! She who reduced our position from nobility to slavery."

Wan'er burst out crying. She wanted to explain to her mother that Wu Zetian was not the woman as described in all the rumours. She had seen Wu Zetian in person. In her eyes she could see that Wu Zetian was a compassionate and astute empress. Her governance had continued the peace and prosperity that she had forged along-side her husband some thirty years earlier. It would be criminal if she wronged a good empress. Why does the ruler have to be a man, as long as the leader does well for the common people? Aside from the fate of her family, Wan'er had a feeling about the dynasty. It was the Tang dynasty that she was attached to, and she hoped for it to be prosperous and happy, and believed that what had passed had passed. She felt wise enough to judge for herself. She kept these thoughts to herself and simply said, "Mother, did I have a choice?"

When Ms Zhen's anger diminished, she moaned, "Why do you treat such an evil woman as your benefactor? It worries me that you go into the court, where one day you are in favour and the next day without a head."

Wan'er replied in a serious tone, "Mother, trust me! I can judge what is right and what is wrong. If Wu Zetian does fit the rumours, and is not good for the common people, I will do my best to oppose her. But if she does what is best for the common people, I will serve her obediently. I will do whatever is the most beneficial for the people in the kingdom. Moreover, by serving her, I can get close to her, find out her weaknesses, and find ways to overcome her. I will make friends secretly, and set up my own secret clique, so that I, too, can gain power".

Hearing her daughter's clear-sighted vision, Ms Zheng relented.

"Mother, you must learn to trust me. Starting from our ances-tors, we have been serving the emperor for generations. I won't let you or the people of the Tang dynasty down."

Ms Zheng nodded her head, though she was still not entirely satisfied.

Chapter Three

Shangguan Zhaoyi

Shangguan Wan'er's reputation as poet extraordinary and talented young scholar spread quickly.

She started her official career by drafting documents and relaying orders to other minor officials.

She served Wu Zetian carefully, neither flattering nor belittling her, keeping her manner respectful, but relaxed, and occasionally sharing some humour together. Step by step, Wu Zetian relaxed her guard around the young girl. Soon, Wu Zetian relied on Wan'er to take on more responsibilities and functions. Wu Zetian cultivated Wan'er carefully, knowing one day Wan'er would be more useful to her.

Though her position was still junior, Wan'er was diligent and enjoyed her various tasks, while learning a great deal from reading and amending classical texts. With her excellent memory, she was able to remember everything she read. Her poetry had even inspired a new literary trend in the Tang dynasty, which was called 'Shangguan style'. She made friends with scholars, where discussions were had about literature and poetry. She enjoyed debate, and was quick to laugh with her opponents. She was generous and open minded, and enjoyed talking to people who held different opinions from her. At the same time, she was realistic and was able to take on any convincing argument. If there was any prejudice she would just laugh it off rather than confront them.

With the greater freedom granted to her by her position, she was able to spend more time in nature. Within nature she was relaxed and enjoyed the mix of quiet and activity it offered. She was expressive, and showed her emotions on her face.

Still, though, there was always the dichotomy of adoring Wu Zetian and her need to avenge her family. There were many times when Wan'er had the chance to murder Wu Zetian. Yet, if she succeeded in killing Wu Zetian, she would be guilty in the eyes of history. Besides, if convicted, she could not serve the court as she did now. She felt there had to be another way. To her great annoyance, she felt Wu Zetian was actually a good empress. She ended up modelling herself on Wu Zetian to a degree, consciously or unconsciously, learning from Wu Zetian's style and even her magnanimity as a great woman. Wan'er considered Wu Zetian to be a real dragon woman. In China, a dragon represents the highest power. Only emperors could be called dragons, and their power was bestowed by God. Wan'er decided she would bide her time and learn.

𡘙 𡘙 𡘙 𡘙 𡘙

A few months later, one scholar said to Wan'er, "The style of literature in the Tang dynasty is full of gorgeous and emotive phrases. The trend at the beginning of Tang dynasty was to write prose full of sumptuous style. People competed against each to create the most extravagant and luxurious pieces, without any real meaning in their writing. I don't think it is good for the future of writing."

Wan'er smiled and replied, "In our time of enlightenment, we must be aware that the wheel of fortune rolls when it reaches the peak. It's better to think of danger in peaceful time, and of peace in troubled times. The golden period, will lead to the downfall of the dynasty."

At this moment, Wu Zetian was passing and overheard their conversation. She asked Wan'er curiously, "I heard what you just said. If you had a greater say, what would you do to do to ensure the continued prosperity of the dynasty?"

"My Empress, I am just an indentured official. I do not dare to comment on political affairs."

"But I just heard you comment on them. Are you so afraid of me that you can't speak your mind? I invite you to continue with your opinion."

"Thank you, my dear Sage Empress. I would think it prudent to enlarge the library of the court, as knowledge will always make people spirituality rich, which is especially important for the people in the court. Secondly, I would increasingly educate the common people in order to select more useful officers for the dynasty." She paused for a second, wondering if what she was about to ask for was too much, "As for myself, I would feel it an honour and privilege to collate and compile an anthology of all the wonderful poetry and prose of the Tang dynasty for you. Should I be entrusted with this beautiful task, I would add notations where relevant. I think this would be a good thing for all lovers of Tang literature, and for the edification of readers in the far future." She then waited with bated breath whilst Wu Zetian considered.

"Are you sure you can achieve this valuable task? After all, as you just said scholars, long in the future will judge us from your efforts."

With the confidence that was beyond her years she said, "I am aware of the value and significance of this task, and humbly will do everything possible to be worthy."

"Very good!" Wu Zetian was satisfied, "Your proposal is granted."

Gradually, Wu Zetian started to promote her protégé. She kept Wan'er by her side, and encouraged her to participate in discussions on governmental affairs and to offer her opinions. At the same time, Wan'er was given more complex and confidential edicts to write. Wan'er was clever and a natural public speaker, debating with insight and finding astute metaphors with ease. It did not take long before many of the older cohort of officials would listen to her speak with interest. When Wu Zetian was not in a good mood, Wan'er was able to pacify her by telling some interesting or humorous story, often from a historical story. Wu Zetian would burst out laughing at her wit, "What a girl you are!"

There was one occasion when Wu Zetian said, "Who would dare to marry you? You little genius. Have you met my son, Tang Zhongzong? What do you think of him?"

Wan'er knelt down and said, "My Empress, in my lowly position, I could never be a judge of the prince. I am just a humble girl."

"Get up! It's just a discussion." Wu Zetian smiled. But Wan'er's heartbeat fast as she did not know whether such a turn of events would be her luck or her misfortune.

ㅋ ㅋ ㅋ ㅋ ㅋ

It was now winter, and huge snowflakes fell from a grey sky, covering all in a white powder. Wu Zetian had gathered together all the court officials at a social event. Wan'er was also in attendance. They were composing poems and linking verses, and there was laughter and goodwill as wine flowed.

Sometimes, Wu Zetian asked Wan'er to adjudicate the poems. There were two famous scholars in the Tang dynasty at that time, Song Wen and Shen Qi. They were equally respected in writing prose and poetry, and both were invited to the banquet.

Wu Zetian, thoroughly enjoying herself, asked all in attendance to write a poem. It could be on any arbitrary theme. She asked Wan'er to judge the best poem.

With their cups full, all attended to their poem. Soon the white sheets flew towards Wan'er, as if large snowflakes falling from the winter sky. When all had finished, she cast a quick glimpse at each of the poems in turn and dropped all but two to the ground. She announced that the two remaining poems were those of the two famous scholars. The contenders and officials were secretly amused, as they were waiting to see if Shangguan Wan'er would make a fool of herself with her pronouncement, as it was believed that the two poets were equally talented. They waited in anticipation.

One official laughed in a pleasant way. He said, "Today, it's our honour to allow Shangguan Wan'er to judge our poems. What a dilemma she has trying to separate the best from the best – Song Wen and Shen Qi – to determine the master poet in Tang dynasty." Wu Zetian heard this and nodded her head approvingly. She was also intrigued as to how Wan'er was going to judge the difference between the two masters.

Wan'er calmly sat on a pavilion chair, looking down at the guests, who in turn watched her with interest. A smiled broke on her face as she let one paper drop to the floor. The closest official hurried to grab the remaining poem from her hand. He announced, "Shen Qi is the winner." There was a rumble of surprise and much whispering. They wondered just how she had come to her decision. Wu Zetian wondered the same thing and asked Wan'er to elaborate. Wan'er smiled and said calmly, "Both poems are brilliant, but Shen Qi's poem shows a more broad-minded picture. Let me explain. In the last sentence of Song Wen's poem, he wrote, *I was as humble as the old trees in the forests, exerting my effort to serve the dynasty wholeheartedly, as previous sages did*. The poem is sincere, but with less life. It read as if an old man was watching the sunset. However, in Shen Qi's poem, he wrote, *I have no fear of the disappearance of the moon, for even in the darkest night I can still find a legendary pearl, which is as luminous as the night*. This poem uplifts the spirit and has greater vitality.

Again there was a buzz of discussion, as all the poems were read aloud. In the end, all had to agree that Wan'er's assessment was the correct one, and that her decision-making process was inspiring.

Wan'er's sagely insight elevated her amongst her peers, and Wu Zetian was so proud of Wan'er that she announced, "So, are all now convinced that Shangguan Wan'er is the most accomplished woman in the Tang dynasty?"

"Yes," was the overwhelming consensus. Thereafter, Wan'er's reputation was well-known throughout the realm, by both the common people and educated classes. She became the de facto judge of all poetry. She was always glad to help, and all were amazed at the breadth of her knowledge and farsightedness. What a spirit she had!

Wu Zetian supported Wan'er in all she did. Wan'er could feel that, and was grateful for the friendship. Gradually her resentment dissipated and she became totally devoted to Wu Zetian and the dynasty. Wu Zetian appreciated this girl for her lofty sentiments and generous behaviour. She believed that there were many men who wished to kneel down and kiss her feet.

ㄱ ㄱ ㄱ ㄱ ㄱ

Winter was coming to an end. The sweet plum flowers announced a new spring. The heavy spring snow promised a good harvest.

Wan'er came to Wu Zetian and said with joy, "Empress Wu, it's snowing outside. Spring snow is a good omen for a good harvest this year. I wonder whether this is a sign of a good luck for our Tang dynasty. With your vigorous effort, our dynasty is flourishing. We all offer our gratitude to you, our Empress."

Wu Zetian was pleased. She said, "Let's go outside, drink and make poetry!"

A group of officials followed Wu Zetian and Wan'er outside. For now it had stopped snowing, and the blue sky only had a few large white clouds. The day was crystal-like in its clarity, and far distances could be clearly seen. The ground was covered with two feet of snow. The tall pines trees had transformed into large white statues. The snow on the petals of the plum flowers formed a beautiful picture – the red stark against white. The beauty of it inspired poetry. Everyone was drinking good wine and talking about literature. With a drink in hand and a slight slur, Wu Zetian enthused, "Ah, the plum flower has announced the arrival of the spring. Why don't other flowers come out to celebrate with us?"

Wan'er, with quick wit said impetuously, "Everything follows the laws of nature. Flowers emerge, and wither again. It is beyond our power to change natural law, not even an empress, who has divine right, can do so. It is impossible for all the flowers to arrive and compete with each other in such cold weather. It is the same for the Tao ruling the dynasty. You can't expect people to have the same voice all the time." Wan'er thought Wu Zetian would appreciate the sentiment.

"What nonsense you talk! How dare you question my authority? If the Plum flower is able to blossom in the early spring, why can't other flowers? Are you hinting that some people in the Tang dynasty are not content with my rule?"

A cloud came over everyone's faces as Wu Zetian turned angry. They all knelt down and murmured in a low but clear voice, "My holy empress, you have governed the kingdom with the previous emperor for more than thirty years, everyone can clearly see your devotion to the kingdom. We all shower you with great respect and gratitude."

Wu Zetian pontificated, "My conscience is clear! I did nothing against my citizens. I tried my best for them, to give them good life. You judge me like this!"

All heads still bowed obediently, they denied the accusations "No...No!"

She continued, "Yes, for more than thirty years, I given my best for the sake of the Kingdom. All of your titles were granted by me. The prosperity of the current time is the result of my continuous effort. Before the previous emperor passed away, he entrusted me to give my son the support he needed. I do not care for titles or power, my whole heart is devoted to the wellbeing of my citizens. In recent years, those who schemed against my rule have suffered for their evil intent. And in the past, the previous prime minister and other high-ranking officials who once had power in their hands were made examples of. Take heed and do not let me down. If any oppose me, they will also be disposed of. If any consider that they are more capable than those dead officials, you are free to rebel against me. Right now... Now!" she screeched. She paused purposely, glaring at the officials bowed at her feet. She continued in the same hysterical way, "If you are not bold or resourceful enough, you will serve me wholeheartedly and respectfully, otherwise all of you will become traitors in the history books."

The officials were unmoving, kneeling with their heads low to the ground. Not a murmur was heard. Many were sweating in the spring chill, afraid that Wu Zetian would pick them out.

"Well?" She screeched.

They murmured in a low voice, "We are devoted to you forever."

She said nothing but went and stood in front of the lowered body of Wan'er "And you Shangguan Wan'er?" She asked sharply.

"I serve you with my whole heart." Wan'er said with a firm voice. She hesitated a little and added stubbornly, "But about the flowers... I meant—"

"Damn those flowers! How dare you question my authority? But for your intellect, you should have been sentenced to jail many times. Don't forget you are the granddaughter of Shangguan Yi, that treacherous traitor. It is I who saved your life out of pity and granted you your current position. Don't ever forget to show your gratitude to me. Remember, I am your benefactor. But I am also your Empress."

"Yes, My Lady."

"In order for you to remember your place, I order that a large plum flower tattoo be placed on your forehead. Since you love plum flowers so much, each time you see your reflection you will remember where you came from. And those who see you will be reminded that it is I who rule this kingdom".

"Thank you, my Empress, for your mercy." Now she knew how quickly the tiger's claws were quick to strike. No one is to be trusted. All pursue power and hide a dagger behind their smile. Wan'er new that she was not safe in the court, and that Empress Wu only tolerated her as a scholar that could be used. She would continue cultivating people to form a clique to support her and help her remain safe.

习 习 习 习 习

Wan'er knew, and it was becoming common knowledge, that Wu Zetian had formed a secret police murder squad out of fear of insurrection, and many of royal blood and other "suspicious" officials had already been done away with. In forming this squad, she had greatly weakened the power of the nobles. She had also promoted weaker officials under her control to fill those positions. At the same time, she placed some new talented officials with integrity in important positions, people such as Shangguan Wan'er. These people were all well controlled by her. For a while, the dynasty was stable, and the economy developed quickly.

Political persecution of those of royal-blood and other nobles continued throughout Wu Zetian's rule. Her son and true ruler, Tang Zhongzong, being of weak will and constitution, was totally controlled by Wu Zetian. As she aged, the empress became more arrogant. To Wan'er's horror, the situation had developed to the extent that it was almost a bloodletting of the city. Wan'er believed Wu Zetian would continue killing until she felt completely safe.

The empress was aware that there were divided loyalties. There were those that supported Wu Zetian, mainly because they feared her. There were those who wanted a male emperor and of royal bloodline. It was clear that Wu's supporting group were larger than the opposing group.

Wan'er may have said yes to supporting the empress, but she really meant no. She hated being 'two-faced', but she had no choice. She needed to survive for the benefit of the dynasty. She had to make alliances with both parties, in order to find support for her advancement. If she did not climb upwards, she would be pushed into the abyss by those who were against her. In her mind there was no turning back. She remained civil and helpful to all she came across, but schemed, knowing that she was in a cat and mouse game. She confided in no one except her mother.

At eighteen years old, she was expert in hiding her thoughts and feelings from Wu Zetian. She was more circumspect, and no longer offered opinions unless directly asked for, and then with caution. She agreed with all that Wu Zetian said. To avoid suspicion, she remained in good humour. As to Wu Zetian, she seemed content with Wan'er's company, and appeared to not sense any discontent in her. Although she was advancing in years, Wu Zetian had no desire to relinquish her hold on power. She applied heavy make up to hide her aging face. None knew her age, and all were too scared to openly speculate.

As Wan'er's power and support base grew, she was able to covertly negotiate and influence situations between the two opposing factions in the court for the sake of the commoners.

Often, though, Wu Zetian did try to privately entice Wan'er into political discourse. Wan'er had no choice but to offer her opinions, however, she was clever enough to tell Wu what she wanted to hear, while managing to pass it off as her own thoughts.

"Do you think our kingdom is the most important in the world?" Wu Zetian asked Wan'er one day.

"Yes, I believe it to be so. After all, there are many foreigners coming to our land to learn our technology and astute ways. They are barbarians, seeking better ways".

"What do you think is the reason for such prosperity in our dynasty?" Wu Zetian asked, clearly testing Wan'er.

"You, madam Empress. Your continuous sage governance places us in the favour of the ancestors. Heaven has blessed us. You have always encouraged the people to plant in the fields, and supported them with wise laws. This year heaven has blessed us with full crops. Moreover, your open trade with foreigners has bought to us much foreign currency. And you have successfully encouraged subordinate kingdoms to pay tribute to us, supplying us with more trade. Our dynasty is really worthy of the title of the Celestial Empire — the brightest and biggest empire. Our kingdom is very strong. The borders are secure. You have kept us safe."

Wu Zetian replied, "Your answers are wise."

In the silence that followed, Wu Zetian glimpsed herself in the mirror. She hated to see her deepening wrinkles, and to see herself growing old. This prompted another question, "Why have you not attempted revenge for your grandfather and father? You have had opportunity enough to kill me, yet you decide to serve me instead?"

Wan'er knelt down and lowered her head. "No, I dare not".

"Why? And when did you give up your anger at me?"

"Do I speak the truth? Or a lie?"

"Naughty! Of course the truth!"

"Since I first studied you, I could see that you are a sage empress. I could see that you have given the best rule to bring happy harmony to all in the dynasty. So I gave up revenge, long ago, and fully submitted myself, under your feet."

"Get up." Though she did not show it on her face, Wu Zetian was pleased. She gently touched the flower tattoo on Warner's forehead as she said, "From now on, you and your mother can move from the slave quarters back to your own residence. I also repeal your slave status… you are both free citizens". She quickly dismissed Wan'er, so as to calm herself down.

Wan'er got up and left. She consciously touched the tattoo on her forehead – her reminder of the claws of Empress Wu. She would never forgive her.

Wan'er could not judge if what had just transpired was auspicious or inauspicious. She would have to watch closely. Certainly, though, it seemed to her that Wu Zetian asked these questions out of self-esteem issues. By now, Wan'er knew Wu Zetian in and out. And she could see that as Wu Zetian aged, she longed for more security in power, and that she became gradually more neurotic and more unreasonable. Having so much blood on her hands for so many years she feared for her own safety. The only way she could ensure her safety was to continue to rule. To this end she had appointed members of the Wu family to official positions, and their influence in the court was beginning to spread.

ㄱㄱㄱㄱㄱ

Her mother, now back in her own home and allowed to do as she wanted, chose to give her daughter all the support she could.

Wan'er was appalled to learn that Wu Zetian had secretly had the name of the temple in her birthplace of Xijing (now modern-day Xi'an) amended to carry her surname, Wu. By doing so, she had elevated herself to the status of a god. This ancient temple, constructed during the Western Han dynasty, had been built to worship the Buddha. Wu Zetian had built several temples in Xijing and other cities, welcoming eminent monks to chant sutras or practicing the religious rites. In the name of filial piety to her mother and ancestors, Wu Zetian made sacrifices to the Buddha, whilst calling for the blessing of the Tang people and the Wu family.

Wu Zetian asked the locals of Xijing to offer sacrifice to her and her family. She also secretly organised for someone to carve her name on a stone, and have it placed near the Luo River. The stone was discovered and bought to the court. The next day, all officials were summoned to the court, where an official, speaking on behalf of Wu Zetian, displayed the newly discovered stone. He said in a loud voice, "From heaven appears a miracle. This stone was found near the river of Luo. On it is the family name of Wu. This surely is a gift bestowed by God. Clearly, the gods have made Wu Zetian of royal blood. She must take the throne as the rightful empress and not just continue to rule on behalf of her son!" At first there was a stunned silence, as suddenly, the whole dynasty was within Wu Zetian's grasp. No one dared to say a word. They quickly recovered and cheered as if a wonderful miracle had just occurred. They knelt down in front of Wu Zetian.

In the year 690, when Wu Zetian reached sixty-six years of age, after years of manipulation, she was crowned empress, and the first female emperor in Chinese history.

In order to legalise her claim throne, Wu Zetian made sacrifice to the Luo river. A large ceremony was held where many leaders from other territories were invited to pay tribute. After that, Wu Zetian proclaimed, "From now on the dynasty will be known as the Zhou dynasty. I am the first female emperor in the new dynasty!"

Everyone knelt down and cheered.

She looked in Wan'er's direction, "Do you know why I use Zhou as the name of the new dynasty, Shangguan Wan'er?"

"My holy Empress, it is because you are born in an ancient family whose root can be traced back to Zhou dynasty. This dynasty lasted for eight hundred years. Zhou was a very prosperous dynasty, so you wish that the new kingdom will be just as prosperous and thus have chosen this auspicious name."

Wu Zetian was satisfied with the reply. She said, "Yes, I can see that you appreciate the truth."

Wan'er knelt down, with a perfect smile on her face, not betraying the emotion in her heart. Wu Zetian said, "Wan'er, prepare the imperial edict immediately." "Yes, my sage Empress."

Wu Zetian again addressed the crowd. "In recognition of this momentous event, I announce a general amnesty! Serious criminals will receive a reduced punishment, and lesser criminals will be pardoned by the court. Court slaves will gain their freedom, and female officials are allowed to return home." Wu Zetian raised her cup and spilled the wine in it onto the floor to propose a toast to God in the heaven. Despite these events, Wu Zetian was not satisfied. She hungered for more power, as if addicted to a drug. And like any addict, she started to lose all rationality, driven by the fear of losing her throne.

Wan'er could also sense Wu Zetian's thirst for power, and was aware of her increasing madness. She was afraid this would be the end of the good days, as her growing need to control would cause chaos. Wan'er was also worried about her own safety in the troubled court. Her alliances with both the royal clan and Wu Zetian's clique were growing. She had found balance between them – but she knew that was not enough, and she would have to tread carefully.

Wan'er worried about the future of Tang dynasty, as she was farsighted enough to see that Wu Zetian would not be safe on the throne, and that the royal nobles would rebel against her faltering rule.

Wan'er was a tactful and skilled diplomat. She was in the centre of the political whirlpool, holding great power in her hands, and was now one of Wu Zetian's closest advisors. Naturally, she was the target of many men. She did have a few romantic attachments with young officials – these helped in strengthening her personal position. These men hunted her, not only for her beauty, but also for her power and influence.

Wu Zetian intended to orchestrate a meeting between Wan'er and Tang Zhongzong. She plotted for Tang Zhongzong to fall in love with Shangguan Wan'er, so that Wan'er would spy on Tang Zhongzong and report back to her.

As spring arrived, the flowers began competing with each other to be the most beautiful, and the imperial garden was full of sweet fragrances. The soft green grass waved in the light breeze, moving as a tide of green waves. The trees were also kissed green by spring. Spring always brought hope to the people, even if the court was in turmoil and complicated political struggle ensued. Spring brought fresh air and hope.

Wu Zetian was so occupied with public work that she seldom had the pleasure to rest or walk in the garden. One day, she asked Wan'er to walk with her in the garden.

"Wan'er, fly my kite. I'm too old to run." A maid passed the kite to Wan'er.

Wan'er obeyed and started to run with the kite. The higher it went the more she laughed. She ran and ran, almost forgetting herself. How enjoyable it was to relax just for a moment! To stay close to nature. If only she was able to fly on the kite, out of the offensive court. Wan'er sighed deeply but quickly recovered from her absent mindedness – reality is very different from imagination. In order to survive, she had to continue striving for power and never stop, in case someone pushed her away from the centre of power. She thought of the kite, unable to escape the fate of being tied to a string. The higher the kite flew, the tighter the string! She grew up in the court, she knew how it worked. If she cut the string, the kite would fall to the ground, and never fly again.

While Wan'er was absorbed in this moment of sentimentality, she collided with a man, Tang Zhongzong, who apparently was just coming to meet his mother Wu Zetian!

"Sorry." Wan'er blushed and apologised. Tang Zhongzong was stunned by the woman in front of him. *What a face, with such a pair of dark brilliant eyes, shining with happiness and peerless wisdom. That rosy mouth, as fresh as the petals of the cherry blossom in the spring.* Her smile was brightened by two vivid dimples. *Oh, she is the girl with the plum flower tattoo on her forehead? Nevertheless, what a peerless beauty!* Tang Zhongzong thought. The twenty-five year old Wan'er, at the prime of her life, glanced upon Tang Zhongzong unsteadily for a moment. She felt a bit giddy.

Tang Zhongzong was a handsome man of average height and build, about forty years old, manly and mature, with a pair of dark eyes. He wore a yellow dragon gown, which seemed a size too big for him. Wan'er's instinct told her that the man in front of him was of good character.

"Wan'er?" Wu Zetian called.

Wan'er hurried to pick up the kite up from the ground and held it back to Wu Zetian. "Yes Madam Empress?" She was still wearing a bright smile on her face.

"This is my son, the Prince, Tang Zhongzong. This is my personal official, Shangguan Wan'er."

In that split second, Wan'er guessed that Tang Zhongzong wanted to restore Tang's prosperity rather than being a puppet emperor.

Tang Zhongzong had long heard of Shangguan Wan'er's reputation as a skilled diplomat and scholar. Never, though, did he expect she had such an innocent and charming face. Her smile would be so rare in the court, where all plotted and schemed. Yet, there was something in Wan'er's character, something deeply hidden and well-disguised. Once discovered, it would shine like a diamond in a crown.

"She is the most talented woman in the dynasty." Wu Zetian said proudly.

"You are joking, my Empress. I am just your humble servant."

"A humble servant? No one in this court writes poetry as well as your do. Your vision is much higher. There were many famous heroines in the past, such as Hua Mulan, who went to war for her father's sake. It was well said that women were not inferior to men. You are certainly not."

Wan'er did not dare to respond to Wu Zetian's remarks, but lowered her head obediently.

"Mother, can I borrow your precious Wan'er? You are too bossy sometimes. I would like to show her some of the city sights. Chang'an has hidden secrets that some don't know of, I would be delighted to show them to Wan'er."

With a sly smile, Wu Zetian joked, "Oh, you are asking for my treasure? How are you going to repay me? Perhaps I should give her to you as a gift? From now on, Wan'er, you are not going to be called by your girlish name. You are to be known as Zhaoyi." (Zhaoyi was a title reserved for the second ranked wives of the emperor, second only to the queen. Prince Tang Zhongzong already had a primary wife, Queen Wei.

"Thank you, my empress." Wan'er kowtowed

Tang Zhongzong was surprised at his mother's generosity. Being so eligible, he knew many women, but had fallen in love with Wan'er at first sight. He knew his mother would not give him something for nothing. Everything had a price – he wondered what it would be.

Who was this Shangguan Wan'er who was suddenly thrust into his life? Nevertheless, Zhongzong pondered that he could not refuse a marriage if his mother ordered it. He bowed to his mother and said, "Thank you my dear mother."

Wan'er was a perceptive young woman with sharp political insight. She was fully aware of what Wu Zetian wanted. Yet, perhaps she herself could gain from such a marriage. She modestly accepted the marriage proposal. The wedding ceremony was in the court palace. Prince Tang Zhongzong and Wan'er kowtowed to Empress Wu, drank wine, and accepted blessings from the other officials who attended. Wan'er's mother had mixed feelings about the marriage, but she kept them to herself.

From the time she met Zhongzong to becoming his wife, it had all happened so fast. Now that it was done, she was bewildered. Wu Zetian's face beamed with satisfaction.

Now married, she hoped she would quickly gain his confidence. She would also coach him in political direction.

There was another concern playing on Wan'er's mind. There were literally thousands of beautiful girls in the kingdom who would fight to become a concubine of an official, but even more so to become a concubine of a prince and rightful emperor. She would have to keep women away from the Prince, because each was a potential set of eyes and ears for Wu Zetian. But not only that, they could influence the Prince in ways that Wu Zetian wanted.

Now she was married, Wan'er started to think of her position among Zhongzong's concubines. His wife, Queen Wei, was the first person Wan'er needed to befriend. Queen Wei was a gracious woman with limited power. Wan'er wanted to get closer to her.

In ancient China, the emperor was able to have many wives. Only the first wife of the emperor was crowned queen. The queen was in charge of the Harem, while the other wives ranked below the queen with different titles and different duties, for example having children. Of course, the lower ranked wives of an emperor had a chance to become the leader of the Harem themselves, that is, if she won the favour of the emperor, or if something happened to the queen, for example she committed a grave mistake or died.

As Wan'er ranked in the second tier of the emperor's wives, she presented herself to Queen Wei several times to gain her friendship, and also to gauge whether her loyalty was to Wu Zetian or her husband the prince. After some time, they grew closer and became friends.

At the same time, as Wu Zetian was aging, and was becoming increasingly cruel. Wu Zetian had announced several harsh public laws that were in the interests of the Wu family, causing a huge protest in the court. It also aroused deep concerns in Wan'er, so she formulated a plan.

Wan'er visited Queen Wei. When she was summoned inside, the queen greeted her warmly, "Oh, Wan'er, it is nice to see you! Thank you for visiting my humble home. You are the freshest flower in the garden at the current time!"

Wan'er bowed and said sincerely and humbly, "I come to visit you to continue our friendship… but also to talk to you on a private matter of urgency. You are a woman of depth, not only kind, but also intelligent".

"Friendship or not, I need to hear what you are here to talk about."

What Wan'er was about to say was the riskiest thing she had done thus far, but after her previous visits she was willing to gamble on the queen's support. "Queen Wei, you are the first wife of Zhongzong, high above the other women in the court, while I am just a humble official. I believe that both of us want to see the dynasty thrive and prosper, but at the moment, Empress Wu holds power. She is becoming more unstable, and her power must be reduced. For the time being, it is expedient that we obey her and keep her trust. Later when the opportunity presents itself, we will find a way to help your husband be restored to his rightful place as true emperor of the Tang dynasty."

The queen also had to be cautious, as she needed to be sure that she could trust Wan'er, "Why are you saying these things? Aren't you Wu Zetian's confidant and friend? Has she not supported your rise in the court and trusted you as one of her closest aides? Why do you suddenly change sides? Or perhaps you just seek to use us to exact your revenge for the murder of your family, and the fact that you were made a slave?"

Wan'er sighed and continued speaking from her heart, "Yes, there was resentment, but I could not let that influence my position. We have to think of the people. I, or we, have no choice. We can all see the darkness that is befalling the dynasty. My grandfather served the Tang dynasty with only the people in mind, and I will do the same. But I know it is not only me. You, and Zhongzong, and many other high-ranking officials, there are many who feel the same way.

I risk my life by talking to you in this way. We have become friends, but this is about more than friendship, it is for the survival of the dynasty. It is also for your husband's sake. He is the rightful ruler."

As Queen Wei took over the tea pouring ceremony, she said, "Aha, it would seem that you have fallen in love with him! I had heard that you are very different from other women. You have trusted me enough to tell me these things. And, as you want to restore our husband's rightful position, you will have my friendship and trust.

I want to hear your suggestions in order to help our husband and the realm''.

Wan'er smiled; her original impression of the Queen was well founded. "I suggest that you remonstrate with the Empress that the laws that she recently announced are too harsh on the citizens. The impact on the dynasty will be drastic. If you consider why China's first dynasty, the Qin dynasty, was overthrown in just a few decades, it was for the same reason. The laws were too demanding of the common people. The people barely survived, and there was famine and hardship. You must have heard through your own network that there is discontent in the court. Now is the right time. If you were to petition Empress Wu for more lenient taxes and kinder policies so as to earn the people's trust once again, not only would it please the commoners, but it would flatter Empress Wu. The government should collect poll tax only until citizens reach the age of twenty-three. Society should promote the ethnic fidelity of our dynasty. It is imperative to reduce the burden of the people, and give farmers more land to plant crops. I'm sure that the Empress will listen to you, and hopefully accept your advice. More importantly, she will likely give you a position of responsibility."

Queen Wei thought Wan'er's suggestions sensible and far sighted.

Queen Wei was an ambitious woman. She was literate, but far less so than Wan'er, and she knew she was inferior to Empress Wu.

Secretly, she aspired to be a ruling Queen, ruling with her husband. Like Wan'er, she needed to wait for her opportunity and bide her time. Queen Wei was astute enough to know that for any of these hopes to come to fruition, she would need the support and direction of Wan'er. She would ensure that she remained friends with her.

Soon after this meeting, Queen Wei paid a visit to Wu Zetian, where she showed respect and obedience towards Wu Zetian before introducing the topic at hand. Wu Zetian listened to what Queen Wei said with interest, but Wu Zetian was suspicious. Queen Wei was not trusted by Wu Zetian, and Wu Zetian felt she was overly ambitious, vain, and scheming, and that she was busy expanding her influence in the court. When listening to her proposal, Wu Zetian was a little surprised that such a woman had become so farsighted. Nevertheless, what Queen Wei said made sense. "You can discuss these measures with my son. If he agrees, then we will make the changes," Wu Zetian said dismissively.

Queen Wei felt a seed of hope had been planted. She retreated and discussed it with Zhongzong, who immediately agreed and announced the amendment of the laws.

Despite the current situation, because of Wu Zetian's tight grasp on power, no one dared oppose her. However, those loyal to the family of the royal bloodline were biding their time.

For the common people there was a sigh of relief. The new laws meant that the people became more loyal to their usually hidden prince. For years there had been a sense of disenchantment with Wu Zetian's reign. They were unhappy about the way she had manipulated the throne away from the royal bloodline, and many wanted the rightful rules to be reinstated. They were also aware of the declining moral and ethical standards of the dynasty. They were keen to play their part if the opportunity arose. Yet, because of the influence of Wu Zetian, the whole dynasty had started to worship Buddha, as she had more and more temples built.

Behind the scenes, Wan'er steadily built up her influence. She had her finger on the pulse of everything that transpired, more so than anyone else. With each mistake the Empress made, Wan'er gained more influence. Still though, she had to continue with great caution.

With so much intrigue, and so many games being play, even Zhongzong secretly watched Wan'er. He needed to be sure of her loyalty towards him and the court. Would she want greater power and betray him and his queen? But gradually he trusted her more and more. He had great respect for her political expertise, and his love for Wan'er was more than just infatuation. He found himself wanting to spend all his spare time with her. When he did, he willingly shared with her his every thought. Wan'er always listened and supported him with a smile and without complaint. She was happy that she was not only treated as a wife, but as his favourite. In return, Wan'er would make up good stories for Zhongzong's sake. She told him a story every night. This time together was treasured by both. Wan'er cherished being adored and worshiped by Zhongzong. For a woman, what else could be more important than winning the respect of her husband?

Zhongzong's spirit was enlivened. He decided to take Wan'er on short journey to visit the Chang Le Princess Palace. He arranged that they travel together in a coach without officials accompanying them. It would seem that it was all romance, but the truth was that he wanted to discuss something important with her.

Wan'er was very beautiful when she laughed. Zhongzong lost himself in her laughter. Wan'er usually laughed without a restrain. He lovingly stared at Wan'er for ages, unable to remove his gaze. He enjoyed her ready wit and wide knowledge.

One evening, after a dinner he said half-jokingly, but with secret desire, "You have the knowledge and ability to govern the court. It's a pity that you seem content to just stay by my mother's side, as her main confidant. What would you say if I were to appoint you as one of my prime ministers?" (In ancient China there were often several prime ministers).

Wan'er was not in the least bit surprised, as she had thought that Zhongzong would make this request eventually. She knew who her supporters would be, and who would be allocated which portfolios once she was in her role. However, at this moment, she smiled, "Do you want me to be your wife, or your official?"

"Ha-ha, I can have many wives, but I lack a prime minister to support me and replace the current Prime Minister Di Renjie, who is too intimate with my mother. Without you, I can do nothing. You must use your talent and serve the people of the dynasty."

"Di Renjie is a good prime minister," Wan'er remarked.

"Indeed, but I need my own prime minster, one I can trust." Zhongzong insisted. "You can be in charge of many things as an imperial concubine."

"It's dangerous to be in so high a position within the court", Wan'er said with concern.

"Let's be frank. Wasn't it your political wisdom and instinct that enabled you to climb so high and stand by my mother's side? And is it not that same wisdom that has ensured that for almost ten years you have remained in that position without being compromised?"

Wan'er instinctively fingered the tattoo on her forehead, and pursed her lips. "Do you really trust me that much?" She needed to be sure of his intentions.

"Why do I trust you? Because I can tell that you are different from my mother. My instinct tells me that it should be you running things."

"Sometimes, instinct cannot be trusted. Nothing is permanent. The world can change in a flash. Today's blossoming flower will fade tomorrow. I could fade into obscurity, with no one to remember me."

"What are you talking about? Of course, nothing is permanent, but you are needed. Worry about now, not tomorrow. Look at your achievements in literature and your political wisdom. You could only become wiser day by day".

"Aha." she sighed. "Maybe you're right. But I can't help feeling a little apprehensive. I have received education in the court, worked and struggled in this arena of politics for the sake of the Tang dynasty. I have been surrounded by cheaters and liars since I was fourteen years old, and I still have to play these games with them."

"My mother is the first female emperor in history, why can't you become the first female prime minister? You can do more than write the imperial edicts for my mother, and write laws for others. You can create the laws. I know you are a close confidant of Wu Zetian, and she listens to what you have to say. But being my wife and a female official at the same time, you would become the brightest star in the Tang dynasty''.

"You flatter me," Wan'er said with a smile.

"You are my favourite wife, but you will need to take on more responsibility as the prime minister. I know it sounds abnormal, but I don't want you to waste your talent by remaining as just my mother's aide. As a prime minster, you could support Di Renjie's work. You would recruit any official you see fit. You would help me make edicts, and we could rule the dynasty together, just as Mother and Father did before he got sick."

"So you want me to do the job of a prime minister, without giving me a title of the prime minster?" Wan'er teased.

"I can give you all the power you need. But because you are my wife it's against tradition to give you a title beyond Zhaoyi."

"I will consider it." Wan'er wanted to keep Zhongzong in suspense.

They went through the gate of the Chang Ning Princess' palace yard and paused adjacent to a pond in the middle of the garden. The pond came from a hot spring located deep underground.

Wan'er was amazed as she stared at the rising vaporous steam. Zhongzong, with a chuckle explained, "This is a hot spring. If you put Lantian jade into a hot spring, it will melt and evaporate into the steam. A bath in a hot spring is very good for a woman's health. We'll bathe later."

Wan'er smiled, "I always wondered how I could keep my beauty from fading. So here is how Empress Wu remained young looking for all these years. After being in government affairs for many years, I will definitely look older than my age, especially if I become a prime minister. I'll be physically and mentally old and tired."

"Why? I would have thought that you would enjoy playing those tricks and political games. You are high in the court, powerful and beautiful, and Empress Wu's aide."

Wan'er smiled. Being a prime minister of Tang Zhongzong, and the having power to control the court, she would have major responsibility over states affairs. As a prime minister, Wan'er's position to influence politics for the benefit of the citizens would be greatly improved.

Wan'er teased him, "As you said, political games are just games. As long as it is a game, the game will come to an end someday. There will always be a winner and a loser. And, when all is said and done, I'll be an old woman, with no one to care for me!"

"I never expect a woman like you would grieve over the changes of nature and be so sentimental."

"Living in the court, everyone is just a chessboard piece. Someone stronger making good moves, while someone weaker gets eaten by their opponents. Sometimes, living and working in the court, I feel surrounded by ambushes. For a small fish like me, all I ever wanted was a place to survive and to read".

With desperation he said, "I will never allow anything to happen to you." As he clutched Wan'er's warm hands in his, he added, "I will exert my power to protect you. I promise. You will be safe".

Wan'er smiled. She could smell the wind of change in the court. Gradually, the family of the royal bloodlines were strengthening their position as Wu Zetian became more demanding and unreasonable. Wan'er did not take Zhongzong's remark seriously. In her opinion, Zhongzong was too weak to fight for his throne. He was just like a new-born chick, whose feathers were not thick enough to fly. However, what Wan'er did know was that he had a lot of resentment towards his mother, and wished to grab back what belonged to him. He was weak in health, but not in mind. He had long been calculating and formed a plan to launch a coup in the court. To this end, he had surrounded himself with like-minded people of influence. He wanted Wan'er to be on his side. He loved Wan'er, and hoped that she would never betray him.

In Wan'er's opinion, many in the court made sacrifices in order to gain something else. When the time came, even Zhongzong, who now made this oath to protect her, would abandon and sacrifice her mercilessly, as if a useless pawn. She long knew the golden rule of survival, that is, to protect herself. Friends could become enemies over night for small gain. She knew she always had to watch her back. However, Wan'er was positive. Most days after waking up, she found the troubles of the past quickly forgotten. She smiled in front of the mirror, seeing her own reflection, wondering whether she had worried too much. Judgement day had not arrived yet. Before that day came, she would enjoy the worldly pleasures of Chang'an city.

Before meeting with the Princess, Wan'er and Zhongzong strolled around the palace garden, where roses of many varieties bloomed. They stopped to admire and smell the different colours. Wan'er loved roses, mentally comparing each flower to a different woman. These flowers, like women, were so tender and fragile and should be loved and treated with tenderness and respect. She saw the parallel with life, where these flowers were able to stand the cold wind and heavy snow of the early spring in order to bloom brightly in full spring.

Wan'er delighted in the garden. The front section was designed with great artistic skill. There were several winding paths leading to secluded dead ends. There were gates that led onto yet more enchanting views. Each of these sections had a different theme, with different varieties of flowers, shrubs and trees. The garden staff, uniquely dressed in traditional uniform, looked as if they were from some distant fairy tale.

They started to cross a bridge but loitered in the middle. The water flowed lazily flowed beneath them, a small stream redirected from the Luo River. There, massive carp leisurely meandered between the lotus flowers, occasionally leaping and splashing about. People fished the ponds, still and silent, waiting for a bite. It was peaceful and Wan'er relaxed into the scene's gentle embrace. For now she could forget all about politics.

They walked further until they reached a wooden palace with red wall surrounding it. It must be the princess Changle's residence, Wan'er thought. Zhongzong smiled at last and said, "Let's go inside and meet the Princess Changle." The servants called Changle when the couple arrived. They waited in one of the living rooms.

Finally, Princess Changle appeared. She was the granddaughter of emperor Tang Taizong, a woman of grace and breeding. A quiet woman who did not talk much, she was nonetheless firm in her opinions. She also longed for power, but she was never able to enter the central power circle of the court. She was depressed and downhearted. In order to forget these troubles, she built this grand palace for herself and was the architect of its gardens. Every day she put on a sun hat and worked the grounds with her servants. Nature gave her joy.

Seeing her visitors, Changle greeted them with a deep bow. She had long heard of Shangguan Wan'er's beauty and reputation. Still, she was stunned. And what was more surprising was that Wan'er did not carry an air of grandeur, even though she had been in such a high position for so long.

Wan'er held Changle's hand as she said warmly, "My dear sister, I have walked your garden. It is so beautiful. I could forever sleep under its trees and never want for anything – you must live a fairy-like life."

Changle was touched by Wan'er's natural demeanour and smiled happily, "If you enjoyed yourself so much, you're welcome to come as often as you want."

"You flatter me." Changle was happy to hear that Wan'er was of the same spirit with nature. All these years she had devoted herself to making this beautiful garden, as consolation for being an invisible woman. The colours and beauty calmed her. Even if she was ignored by Empress Wu, she was still satisfied with her life, as she was not alone. Wan'er's comments immediately won Changle's trust.

Both Zhongzong and Wan'er were quick to thank the princess' generosity.

Later, they returned to the garden. Surrounded by such beauty, Wan'er felt inspired. She said to Zhongzong, "I have some poems to write."

Zhongzong hurried to tell a servant to bring paper, ink and a brush.

Wan'er composed twenty-five poems on that visit. This was one of them:

Strolling the Chang Ning palace,
enjoying heaven's view,
I find it hard to express my feelings
swarming with perplexity
hard to describe it with a brush.
I crossed one palliation after another.

I climbed the Peng Lai Mountain near the river.
I came into the Lu house,
where the dragon air of the Qin dynasty was sealed by
the Han emperor.
The high mountains and the strong wall surround
flowers blooming blooming.
Bamboo sways in the gentle breeze,
Whispering pine trees "ssshhhhhh", sunlight on
their needles
music from heaven.
Pleasure replacing pain.
Looking down, at the cottage nearby,
the tree branches hang on the hillside,
the rosy glow of the sky
as if the breeze and moon cared for me.
The leaves on the trees green,
so funny and gentlemanly.
The forests on the mountain are my company,
the pines and sweet flowers my friends;
I walked nearer, and nearer
lost, lingering.
Where else is as refreshing and carefree?
This fairy land.....

Watching intently, Zhongzong asked, "Have you finished?"

Wan'er did not respond, as she sat near the pond, hearing the bubbling sound of the water dancing across stones – music from heaven. She continued writing.

He sat by her side, saying nothing, silently supporting her. As he watched her, he could not help admire Wan'er's poetical talent. "Your lines are so touching. I imagine if you decided to abandon your title, I see you living the life of a reclusive scholar in a mountain temple. The last few lines revealed your true ambition."

"What makes you think so?"

"You wrote: *walking further in the garden of the*
palace,
encountering different dangers,
the toes of my feet too painful,
My heart, stilled with happiness,
in this high retreat.
Pine leaves, frozen, white,
as sweet as jade.
Oh, to live here!
Day and night,
eating leftovers, I would be content.
And would play the Guqin...'

"Is this not your ambition revealed here? What an open minded woman you are! I revel in your words!" He giggled with emotion, "How do you get inspired? The style of your poetry is so different from your decisive actions... a different aspect of your character, from that in the court".

Wan'er hated being intruded upon and suddenly felt an urge to cry, but she restrained herself, as usual, ever the diplomat. It was better not to expose her feelings, even to someone so intimate, for every word she uttered could be used as a weapon against her. Composed, she said, "Maybe it is because I grew up in the court that nature is so attractive to me. I enjoy seeing the different moods of the four seasons, to walk around in the garden. But fate has decided my path. I could never abandon what fate has determined for me. Sometimes there are no choices. Don't you think?"

"Yes, we have choices." Zhongzong refuted her eagerly. "All of us have a choice. We are the masters of our own fate. It is by our own free will that we decide whether we are happy or unhappy."

"But how?" Wan'er did not understand, especially when she considered how his mother has impinged upon his life so severely.

"By asking your heart for what you really want and then following it." Zhongzong said half smilingly and half seriously. He put his hands on Wan'er's heart. She felt its strong beat.

Zhongzong became quiet, sinking into deep thought – mapping out the political situation in his mind. According to his father's last edict, issued on his deathbed, his mother Wu Zetian was to support him. Instead, she claimed all power, even manipulating the law so that she could become the so-called "legal" Empress. Zhongzong often had nightmares. In his dreams, his mother was draining his blood. He always woke up at the same point in the dream. Did he himself have a choice? Would he prefer to be the puppet emperor of his mother for as long as she lived? Or would he stand up and fight for his rightful heritage and destiny?

Wan'er could not know what he was thinking. She smiled innocently, "None of us can ever be free from our duties and escape from this world. A common hermit can live in solitude; a good hermit knows what he wants. A real hermit lives in the court. Some people are schemers and are cunning, but are good and upright in their heart. In order to survive they cover their heart in a hard shell so that no poison can harm them. Their behaviour will be judged by history at the end of their life."

She was thoughtful, her eyebrows knitted together, and then she raised her head high and said decisively, "If you think

I should be the prime minister, I will take on that position, despite you not giving me an official title. But first tell me, how are you going to convince the Empress?"

"I will simply ask her." Zhongzong laughed. "I am confident that she will agree."

They continued to walk and came to a stop at the hot spring.

Wan'er gazed at the spring in a wonder. Perceiving her interest, Zhongzong said, "Let's swim".

Wan'er removed her grown and sunk into the water. Within a few minutes she was totally relaxed. When Tang Zhongzong went in, they splashed and paddled happily, forgetting all talk of politics as they laughed and splashed the afternoon away.

ㅋ ㅋ ㅋ ㅋ ㅋ

That evening, after an agreeable conversation between the three of them, Zhongzong became serious and said to the princess Changle, "I have decided to appoint Wan'er to do the duties of the prime minister of the court."

"You are sure that you want such a beautiful wife to be a prime minister?" Changle laughed, rather surprisingly.

"Ah, this is my fate." Wan'er said, whilst shrugging her shoulders.

"I'm sure Empress Wu won't be against my proposal. Anyway, she probably knows of Wan'er's ability better than anyone."

Wan'er smiled. She knew it was true. She also knew that Wu Zetian still trusted her, and that she would still have to act as if she were spying on Zhongzong. Moreover, as Wu Zetian grew old, she believed that Zhongzong's plan would work.

ㅋ ㅋ ㅋ ㅋ ㅋ

Wu Zetian also had a daughter, a princess called Tai Ping. In Chinese, this name means safe and sound. Tai Ping was her mother's favourite. She was very much like Wu Zetian as she was also bossy and arrogant, always striving to gain more from everyone. Wu Zetian privately discussed political affairs with Tai Ping. By doing so she taught her about the court. Even so, she kept the Tai Ping in the shadows. This aroused rebellion in Tai Ping. Tai Ping lost patience, as time and tide waited for no man or woman. She secretly established many connections in the court. Her brother, Zhongzong, took advantage of this situation and plotted with his sister. Together, they both bided their time, while hoping for the right opportunity to come along.

う う う う う

And so Zhongzong proposed to Wu Zetian to that Wan'er take on the duties of a second prime minister. With this proposal, Wan'er's power was beyond that of both the Wu family and the royal family. Strangely enough, Wu Zetian was not against it. With the request from Zhongzong, Wan'er was elevated, though still without the title of prime minister. She not only had real power in her hands, but also ranked highly because of her status as Zhongzong's wife and advisor. Wu Zetian knew of Wan'er's ability to rule, and trusted Wan'er to be loyal to her. Wu Zetian accepted the proposal.

う う う う う

Wan'er kowtowed and thanked Wu Zetian for the promotion. When she told her mother of her pending promotion, Ms Zheng just smiled contently, but did not comment much. Wan'er assured her that she would do her best for the people of the Tang dynasty.

The announcement was made and the ceremony was held. Wu Zetian continued to ask Wan'er if she had any new information on

Zhongzong, and showed every sign of believing what Wan'er told her.

One day, when they were both sitting together, Wu Zetian suddenly said, "Wan'er, you are now in the position your grandfather once held. How do you feel? I hope you will not let me down."

Wan'er was surprised at Wu Zetian's question, but she kept calm, lowered her head, and said, "I appreciate all you have done for me. I won't let you down."

These days, Wu Zetian was always tired and was starting to feel her age. The struggle to hold on to her power exhausted her. She waved her hands and dismissed Wan'er.

彐 彐 彐 彐 彐 彐

As prime minister, Wan'er was active and took many measures to help govern the country. Nevertheless, she continued her work in amending the books of Tang dynasty as she loved doing this work. She also took measures to enlarge the court library. All the famous poems and prose of the Tang dynasty were collated. In her own study, she had also collected many famous ancient books, including the Confucian classics, different historical volumes of previous dynasties, and tomes of philosophy and literature. Historical volumes of previous dynasties were the focus of her work. She paid more attention to the lost dynasties, including the Liang, Northern Qi, Northern Zhou, and Sui dynasties. She endeavoured to keep the record of historical facts accurate, as, in her opinion, history had the habit of repeating itself. By reading history, people could learn from the past, judge right from wrong, and avoid making the same mistakes as those from previous eras.

She focused on promoting scholars with good ability, as she felt their skills should be utilised. Wan'er was encouraging and open towards these newly selected officers, willing to hear different opinions, even though in many cases these officials did not have any family connections and were promoted against tradition. In charge of education, Wan'er expanded the scale of the court school, allowing four top scholars to teach students together with eight assistant scholars, and twelve common masters. The masters had to be the most erudite scholars. When her husband learnt of this, he changed the name of the court school to Zhaorong School to honour Wan'er, as Zhaorong was another form of title for emperor's wives in the Tang dynasty.

Zhongzong asked Wan'er, "Do you want to teach literature in the school?" Wan'er smiled confidently, "No, not really. I would like all scholars to teach the students in the area of study in which they specialised." Under Wan'er's continuous effort, the regulations of the Imperial exams were upgraded. People who passed the examination would be invited to serve the court. She tried to encourage men of wisdom and virtue from all over the dynasty to enter the court. Suddenly, the Tang dynasty was benefitting from its own renaissance and flourished with creativity. Some people, though, became arrogant, and offered uncalled for opinions. Wan'er would laugh off those that offended her, but she was receptive to those who dared to point out her mistakes.

At the same time she maintained her reputation as a leading poet, setting the trend and style of the time. Wan'er's poetry was emotive towards nature, with artfully chosen words and a fresh expression.

When the Zhaorong school was finished, Wan'er led Zhongzong to inspect the expanded court school. Wan'er showed him the library and the books that she was amending. By now, Wu Zetian was too old to deal with political issues. The other prime minister and Wu Zetian's friend, Di Renjie, had died. It was a shock for Wu Zetian and caused her much pain, as he was an upright and knowledgeable man, who dared to remonstrate with her wholeheartedly. The death of Di Renjie sent Wu Zetian into deep grief. She was seldom seen in the court thereafter. Zhongzong took greater control. He granted almost all of Wan'er's proposal, fully admiring and appreciating her vision and judgement.

As Wan'er was in such a high position, many men tried to get closer to her in order to be promoted quickly, or gain commissions from the court. They enticed her with sex, wealth and deals. However, she was too clear thinking and smart for that, and played them to retain their loyalty and use them to their fullest potential. Gradually, Wan'er promoted several officials according to their ability, but those who fished for fame were not allowed an appointment. She was aware that those whom she rejected could seek revenge, as these people were descendants of powerful families. She only did what she thought was best for the dynasty, but dealt carefully with the relatives of both the royal family and the Wu family, trying to balance the interests of both clans.

Wan'er made friends with Wu Zetian's nephew Wu Sansi, and in doing this won the greater trust of Wu Zetian. The now old Wu Zetian was satisfied with her two female hands – the princess Tai Ping, who she had kept in the shadows, but now had more power and unbeknownst to the empress was scheming with her brother against her; and Wan'er, who fed her a lot of useful information. At the same time, there were also Empress Wu's two trusted male officials who helped her eliminate those who schemed against her.

When they discovered their common interest, princess Tai Ping and Wan'er became allies and supported Zhongzong's claim to the throne.

Wu Zetian had little energy to fight back and confined herself in her rooms, refusing to see anybody.

Because she understood Zhongzong's character and ambition, plus all the intrigue that had overtaken the court, she believed that one day another political drama would engulf Tang dynasty. Wu Zetian waited, and observed everything happening around her with calculating demeanour, but now as an outsider, rather than an insider.

The next year, Zhongzong launched a coup in the court and finally grabbed the throne from Wu Zetian. Wan'er was not on the list of the people who would face punishment; on the contrary, he kept Wan'er in the important position of prime minister for almost thirty years.

For the remaining years of her life between 677-705 AD Wu Zetian retired from the throne and became the grand empress dowager in name only.

Chapter Four

The death of the female prime minister

Politics in those times was a dangerous game. Most did not survive its ebbs and flows, and many had no faith in politics. However, Wan'er was different. Her life-long-tragedy was that she was idealistic, but reality was quite cruel. Wan'er was so principled that even though she was born the natural enemy of Wu Zetian, she still served her enemy to the best of her ability. She was the same with her husband Zhongzong, who in many ways opposed his mother. But, being married to him, she devoted herself to helping and supporting him. As a female prime minister, she stood with him, shoulder to shoulder as a wife and aide, to care and love him. Of course, as is the nature of politics, she made enemies during her ascent, and lost the trust of many.

She knew she was in a precarious position, and that her career and life were in danger. Being the emperor's wife was not enough to survive political games, especially as it was known that she had been Wu Zetian's aide and confidant for so many years. Yet, she did what she felt was in the best interests of the dynasty. She was afraid that with Wu Zetian's controlling influence gone, there would be another reign of terror in the court. When Zhongzong announced his heir, the Wu side of the family was up in arms, and so a greater confrontation within the royal bloodline occurred.

Wan'er could not help recalling memories of the past. The years had taken their toll, and, deep in her mind, she was weary and bored. She reminded herself that sometimes after happiness, sadness followed. She had little time for romance or self-indulgence as she had been fully involved in politics since she was fourteen.

For the common citizens, they did not care whether the dynasty that they lived in was called Zhou or Tang. For them, their only concern was that they could feed themselves and their family, could find shelter and warmth in winter. Wu Zetian and Zhongzong were from the same royal family, mother and son, fighting a war among themselves. It did not matter to them.

ㄱ ㄱ ㄱ ㄱ ㄱ

When a woman's beauty fades, men's heart change. In the blink of an eye, reaching the age of forty, Wan'er lost Zhongzong's favour, and he married a new concubine, one who was much younger and sweeter. He was indulged fully in this latest conquest.

In order to win more living space and survive in this deeply troubled court, Wan'er made full use of Wu Sansi, Wu Zetian's nephew, for her own safety. As one of the empress's relatives, Wu Sansi held some power, and had many official connections. He was bossy and flattering when it suited him. She purposely introduced him to Queen Wei, and he immediately won the Queen's trust.

Queen Wei also felt deserted by Zhongzong, so she warmly received friendship from Wan'er. "Thank you for caring." Said Wan'er to Queen Wei, and the two remained allies at that time.

"It doesn't matter. We are both women. For what reason shouldn't we become friends?" Queen Wei patted Wan'er's hands softly and said. "Without you as prime minister, anything could happen in the Tang dynasty!"

Wan'er smiled faintly and said, "I have to rely upon you totally, my dear queen. I have no friends or relatives in this court, only you. I hope I can continue to serve you."

When she was in her own room, Wan'er hoped Zhongzong would come to visit. She could not help but be saddened by her loneliness. How could she, such a talented and pretty woman, bear such humiliation? She felt great fury. How stupid she was to lock herself into her chamber and expect Zhongzong to come to her. Men were faithless and could not be trusted. She shivered when she remembered all his fine words. No wonder emperor Wu Zetian wanted to become an emperor herself! If a woman was on top, she didn't need to look at other people's faces. On the contrary, everyone would kneel down in front of her and kiss her feet. It was Wu Zetian who played with men's feeling, but no man dared to play with her feelings. Wu Zetian was a remarkable woman! Without Zhongzong in the room, it looked empty and shabby. She needed care and tenderness from her husband. What was the use of having so much power in her hands when each night she faced loneliness? From her window she looked at the silver moon. *I was right to give up revenge,* she thought to herself. *I hope Zhongzong could understand how it feels to be discarded!* Wan'er clenched her jaw with sadness. She wanted to punish Zhongzong by sleeping with other men in the same way that he had abandoned her.

One night, Wan'er changed her clothes into those of a man's to hide her identity. She rode a horse out of the palace to a cottage near the Luo River. She was free to come and go, as she was the female prime minister. She had made an appointment with Wu Sansi to meet him there. Together they stayed the night, made love, drank wine, and laughed hysterically, until twilight entered the window. Wu Sansi hungrily touched Wan'er's soft and pale body. He kissed her with glee, sucking her fragrance from her, fully intoxicated.

As Wan'er dressed, she said to Wu Sansi, "Remember Queen Wei, whom I introduced to you?"

"Yes, of course."

"I want you to make friends with her and take advantage of the opportunity to crowd out the Emperor's clique in the political arena. Do you know what I mean?"

"I understand." Wu Sansi hugged Wan'er's slender waist and gave her a sweet kiss.

ꓱ ꓱ ꓱ ꓱ ꓱ

Queen Wei had a daughter with Zhongzong, whose name was Anle. Queen Wei admired Wu Zetian's femininity, and she wished her daughter would become a second Wu Zetian. Queen Wei wanted to draw Wan'er to her side, taking advantage of Wan'er's talent and making full use of Wu Sansi's connections, to balance the power with Zhongzong's clique. Wu Sansi, with Queen Wei's help, shed blood, royal blood. Wu Sansi acted as an assassin for them to intimidate Zhongzong and gain control of him. However, Zhongzong was too blind to see that Queen Wei and Wu Sansi were flirting with each other in the court.

Wu Sansi had killed or expelled several powerful and honest officials from of the court. The power-play reverted back and forth, and Zhongzong's clique was gravely weakened, a bird without wings.

Zhongzong, always of a sickly constitution, declined in health not long after he had gained power from his mother's hands. He realised that he could not escape the political game because he was of royal blood. There was so much going on, but he thought of none of it. On his death bed there was a shadow in his heart. It was the shadow of Wan'er. The times he had spent with Wan'er were his fondest memories. He saw her smile, her generosity and vivacious character. Everything about her made his memories taste sweet. He simply could not give her up. Wan'er was a real woman, despite being a prime minister and older. He closed his eyes, two streams of tears flowing from his cheeks. He called for her.

When seeing the bony, sallow face of Zhongzong, tears brimmed in her eyes.

He tried to catch Wan'er's hands and said, "Wan'er, I'm old, but you are still young. I want you to answer me honestly. Look into my eyes. How many love affairs have you had? Am I the most important man in your life?"

Wan'er was astonished. She did not expect Zhongzong to confront her directly.

"None," Wan'er lied – the memories of her affair with Wu Sansi made her break out in a cold sweat. She could not tell him the truth on his deathbed. She also remembered with resentment Zhongzong's abandonment of her.

He smiled and let it go, "If you say so, I believe it be so. I summon you to ask for advice."

"Please."

"Who is more suitable to be the heir to the throne? Crown Prince Li Chongjun (who was the rightful heir, but was side-lined by Queen Wei) or princess Anle?"

Wan'er felt a pang in her conscience. For the first time in Wan'er's life she regretted supporting Queen Wei. She wanted to see the prosperity of the Tang dynasty continue, but was afraid that it may split apart after Zhongzong's death. She said with concern, "Not Anle. She must not be your successor."

"Why?" Zhongzong was surprised at her ferocity. He had thought Wan'er liked Anle.

Her eyes were filled with determination as she rallied, "Queen Wei is a very ambitious woman, who wants to achieve success by any means. It's obvious that she wants to be another empress like Wu Zetian. If you made Princess Anle your successor, the royal bloodline will launch a coup. The dynasty would be shaken like a house in a storm. Moreover, you couldn't convince all of the officials to make Anle your successor. She is impulsive, shallow, vindictive, and has a dangerous yearning for power. Do you know why your mother was so afraid of the legitimacy of her throne?"

"Why?"

"Because the people are devoted to the royal bloodline, not to the relatives of the emperor!"

"Oh, you think so? But still, I don't want to change my mind. Who said another female can't be an empress? What man could outsmart you in court?"

"But neither Anle nor Queen Wei are your mother."

"I can't see that."

"Then you are blind." The words burst out of her mouth angrily. For a moment, Wan'er was worried. She secretly prayed to God to allow Zhongzong to open up his eyes and judge her more sensibly.

Wan'er knew he was being stupid. She wanted to slap his face, to wake him up. She stood up, unfastened her hair, picked up a knife, and said, "If you don't listen to me, and insist on making Princess Anle your successor, I will resign from my official post and cut off my hair to become a nun!"

He was shocked by Wan'er's fierce response. He seldom saw Wan'er lose her temper. He could be wrong, but he refused to admit it.

She replied, "I'm tired, and I give up. Create your own ruin. It's time to retire from my position!" With these words, Wan'er quickly left the room.

Queen Wei quickly got the news that Zhongzong had summoned Wan'er to his deathbed. It was also known that they had a long conversation. What was more dramatic was that when Wan'er left Zhongzong chamber, people saw her with her hair down. They could see her deep anguish. This made Queen Wei suspicious and alarmed. It was obvious to her that Wan'er was never really on her side, and behaved just like grass on the top of a wall, swaying in the wind, this way and that. In these times, nobody could really trust one another. There was no friendship, not even between women. Queen Wei suspected that Wan'er was taking measures to prevent her from gaining the throne.

Anle, too, was eager to get the throne. At this critical point, she was anxious to see what the last edict from Zhongzong would be. Anle asked her mother, "What should we do? If the young Prince Li Chongjun is crowned as the emperor, we will be killed!"

An idea occurred to Queen Wei at this critical moment. People always act out of fear in order to gain more power. Queen Wei said, "It's better to gain the upper hand by acting first."

"What do you mean?" Anle asked anxiously.

Queen Wei smiled wickedly and said, "Never mind, I will arrange everything."

Then she whispered something into her intimate eunuch's ears, who nodded his head knowingly and went away.

Zhongzong was still sick in bed, confused. He pondered Wan'er's words. He could not forget how angry Wan'er was. He sighed. But could he trust her? Suddenly, he felt a sense of jealousy sweeping his heart. He knew all about her love affair with Wu Sansi. Did she think he was a fool? With these jealous and indignant thoughts, Zhongzong wrote his last edict. He decided to pass the crown to Anle. This last effort tired him out.

At this moment, a eunuch was brought in carrying a basket. "My lord, Queen Wei has cooked a lovely black-bone silky fowl for you. It contains Chinese yam and Chinese skullcap. It will be good for you, invigorate your blood, and nourish the Qi in your body."

"Leave it on the side here." Zhongzong said, waving his hands weakly.

"Please don't let Queen Wei down." The eunuch urged and coaxed him to eat it immediately, "Queen Wei came to the kitchen and cooked it herself. She is so worried about your health."

Zhongzong was deeply touched. For a man who had just been hurt by a strong-minded woman, another woman's tenderness was welcome. Zhongzong struggled to get up and ordered the servant to feed him.

After finishing the soup, Zhongzong felt his head swirl. He sank into a deep sleep. The next day he was found dead!

Everyone was shocked at Zhongzong's sudden death at the age of fifty-five. Wan'er nearly fainted when she heard the news. She had to be supported by her servants into her chamber to lie down. When she woke up, her servant told her that it had been announced that Anle was to be the next empress. Hearing this, Wan'er cried out in anguish, "Aaaah!"

Her reasoning told her it was murder. It was all her fault by befriending Queen Wei and excluding the prince's clique from the court. It was also she who whipped up this situation by speaking ill of the prince to Zhongzong so. Having poison hidden in her bed chamber, she retrieved it and drank it. She waited for her own death.

ㄢ ㄢ ㄢ ㄢ ㄢ

Wan'er wondered where she was. She heard someone calling her name and gradually opened up her eyes. Her blurred vision clearing enough to see Queen Wei sitting beside her, "My sister, why do you seek suicide? Our Tang dynasty needs you as the prime minister."

The death of the female prime minister 139

Though she was suspicious that Wan'er had betrayed her, she had no evidence to support it. Moreover, the court would stop operating without Wan'er. Hearing Wan'er was poisoned, or possible try to commit suicide, she suppressed her anger, and decided to try and save her from death.

Wan'er was too weak to reply, but smiled faintly.

"Your situation is the same as Zhongzong's. The doctor said that he was also poisoned by someone, but has no clue as to who that person is. I have given you an antidote, but you are still in danger." Queen Wei patted Wan'er's hands warmly to comfort her. Wan'er's life would be in danger if Queen Wei knew of the nature of the conversation between herself and Zhongzong, yet the Queen was trying to save her.

"Thank you, my dear queen. I will forever be your faithful servant." Wan'er tried to make a gesture to bow, but was stopped by Queen Wei. Queen Wei said, "There is no need for modesty between sisters."

Wan'er managed a false smile, wondering whether if she survived, she would be able to escape her fate in this drama.

ㄱ ㄱ ㄱ ㄱ ㄱ

After Wan'er introduced Wu Sansi to Queen Wei, Wu Sansi was put in charge of the court. Wu Sansi's son married Anle, and gradually gained more control over the court. With the help of Queen Wei, he had killed many dissidents in the court.

Wu Sansi encouraged Wan'er to continue their relationship, but Wan'er closed her door to him. At the same time, Wu Sansi also romanced Queen Wei, and together they had their opponents killed to strengthen their power.

A drought had struck the kingdom and the common citizens suffered much hardship. Queen Wei had no idea what to do for them or the dynasty. She sought Wan'er's help. Wan'er declined, saying she was too ill. She suggested, with irony, that she ask Wu Zetian for help, or beg the gods for rain. Queen Wei left the room angrily to discuss the issue with Wu Sansi.

While Wan'er was sinking deep into memories and regret, she often thought of Zhongzong. He sometimes appeared in front of her eyes, or in her dreams. Wan'er would try to apologise, but he would disappear. There was no remedy for that. With tears filling her eyes, line by line, Wan'er wrote her last poem on her sickbed:

Boudoir complaints in letters;

I still can't forget

the first time we met.

It was spring,

golden leaves falling from the trees,

nearby, Dong Ting lake.

Thousands of miles away from each other.

Apart forever,

my love sickness endures.

The dew in the autumn is too cold and sad.

The cover on my body too thin to keep me warm.

The silver moonlight shining through the window,

on the pillow on my bed.

Alone,

I can't find you – anywhere.

The vast sky empty and dull,

I wish to sing the song of joy to the south.

However, I can only write a letter to the north.

With nothing in the letter,

but full of memories of you.

In 710 AD, Shangguan Wan'er, at the age of forty-six, was sick, but alive. She tried to ignore political affairs, leaving Wu Sansi and Queen Wei to run the court. Tai Ping's gradually grew stronger. Different parties competed in the court, and fought for the throne. They all secretly developed their own followers and were all locked in open struggle. After Zhongzong's death and years of struggle, Wan'er's talents were exhausted by the sorrows and countless plots in the court. Queen Wei wanted to follow Wu Zetian's example and hold all power to herself. But Wan'er was afraid that the Tang dynasty would be ruined by this woman's hand, so she used all her strength and dragged her poor body to visit Tai Ping to suggest a plan.

At this point, Tai Ping had the greatest control over the court. Wan'er said to her, "The Tang dynasty is crumbling. We must do something."

"But all the palace guards are under the control of Queen Wei and Wu Sansi. What can we do?"

Wan'er said, "There is a way... Li Longji, Wu Zetian's grandson, being of royal blood, will never allow Queen Wei and Wu Sansi to destroy the court and persecute his people. If prompted, he would surely attack the palace. We must make a false edict in Zhongzong's name, announcing his legitimacy to the throne."

"Will this work?"

"We must try it."

They hurriedly wrote an edict in Tang Zhongzong's name. With this move, Li Longji was free to enter the political scene.

As Wan'er had predicted, Li Longji indeed led an army to attack the palace. Li Longji's army fought hard with Queen Wei's palace guard. Much blood was shed in the palace. The city walls were broken and the whole city was black with smoke. A large part of the palace was ruined. Wan'er waited nervously in her chamber, praying with a nervous heart. After hours of fierce fighting, Li Longji was victorious. When Li Longji entered the palace, Wan'er ordered the palace maids to stand in two opposing lines, with one candle in each hand, showing Li Longji that he was welcome.

Wan'er went to Li Longji, knelt down and passed the false imperial edict to him. Li Longji was delighted. He sighed secretly because of Wan'er's extraordinary beauty and talent. It was a pity to have to kill her. His adviser Liu You suggested, "Save Shangguan Wan'er's life. She has done many good things for the common people for many years while she was the prime minister."

Li Longji said nothing, but dropped the imperial edict to the floor. Giving a signal, a guard arrested Shangguan Wan'er.

习 习 习 习 习

The dynasty's name was changed back to the Tang Dynasty. Li Longji became emperor and became known as Tang Xuanzong, the successor of the royal blood line. He knew that Shangguan Wan'er was innocent, but she was a victim of politics. Wan'er was forced first to support Empress Wu, then her husband Tang Zhongzong. It was also widely known that she was one of Wu Sansi's lovers and friend of Queen Wei. She had tried to find the balance between different political parties, however, that was just fantasy. From the very beginning, after Wu Zetian killed her father and grandfather, and cultivated her as a useful political tool, Shangguan Wan'er was never able to be free of her destiny.

Sometimes, Li Longji wondered whether he had indeed made a mistake, knowing that Shangguan Wan'er was innocent. He visited Shangguan Wan'er's school in the court, finding it was well organised and disciplined. He opened the history books, which she had edited, surprised to find that such a woman had so much talent for history and poetry. Li Longji felt a deep sense of nostalgia, sighing for the unfair fate of this woman. He wanted to do something to memorialise this most legendary woman, and had her title as Shangguan Zhaoyi reinstated. He ordered that her works, and poems be collated and placed in one book, which was titled *The poetry of Tang dynasty* by Shangguan Wan'er.

Biography:

Shangguan Wan'er (644 AD-710 AD): Born in Henan province, prime minister during the Tang dynasty in responsibility but not in name, a poet, and the wife of the Prince Tang Zhongzong. She grew up in the court as a court slave because her grandfather (Shangguan Yi) had cautioned the emperor, Tang Gaozong, not to appoint Wu Zetian as the empress to support their son.

Shangguan Wan'er received promotions from Wu Zetian because she showed her talent at a very young age. She took on the task of updating and ratifying the history books, she was put in charge of the court school, and she wrote imperial edicts for Wu Zetian. She took many measures that would benefit the people.

In order to stay firm in the court, Shangguan Wan'er had several affairs with other men, including Wu Zetian's nephew Wu Sansi. Together with Princess Tai Ping, they schemed to reclaim the throne for Li Longji. She was strongly against the throne going to Princess Anle.

In 710 AD, Li Longji raised an army, entered the court and became emperor. He sentenced Shangguan Wan'er to death.

Wu Zetian (624 AD-705 AD): Born in Shanxi province, she was a politician in the Tang dynasty. She was the first female empress in Chinese history and changed the name of the Tang dynasty to the Zhou dynasty.

Wu Zetian entered into the court at the age of fourteen. She was the wife of Tang Gaozong and was given the title of Mei Niang. In 655 AD, Tang Gaozong deposed the sitting queen, and made Wu Zetian the queen. She governed the court with Tang Gaozong, as Tang Gaozong was not in a good health. Wu Zetian gradually gained power in the court. When Tang Gaozong died, Wu Zetian attended to state affairs behind a screen, while her sickly and weak son Tang Zhongzong was fully under her control.

In 690 AD, Wu Zetian became the empress. She imposed several good measures and edicts. However, as she grew old she became cruel.

In 705 AD, Tang Zhongzong made a change in the court. Wu Zetian's title was changed to Queen Mother. She died not long after this change.

Tang Gaozong (628 AD-683 AD): Named Li Zhi, the third emperor of the Tang dynasty. He became the crowned prince in the year 643 AD, and in the year of 649 AD, he became emperor. His official name as ruler was Tang Gaozong.

At the beginning of his governance he was supported by many senior officials due to his diligent governance. In the year 600 AD, Tang Gaozong fell sick. It was difficult for him to continue governing the court alone, and Wu Zetian gradually took control. Before Tang Gaozong died he made his final edict that Wu Zetian should govern in conjunction with their son, the prince.

Shangguan Yi (608 AD-665 AD): Born in Henan province. The prime minister of the Tang dynasty during Tang Gaozong period, he was a poet and the grandfather of Shangguan Wan'er.

When he was young, Shangguan Yi was a monk. Later, he passed the Imperial examination and entered the court as an official. His position kept rising and in the year 662 AD, Shangguan Yi was honoured as the prime minister of the Tang dynasty. However, in the year 665 AD, he persuaded the emperor to remove Wu Zetian as the empress. By doing so he became her enemy. He was sentenced to death in the name of rebellion. However, miraculously, the life of his daughter and granddaughter were saved, but they were rendered court slaves.

Tang Zhongzong (656 AD-710 AD): Named Li Xian, the fourth emperor of the Tang dynasty. At the beginning of his reign, Li Xian was the crown prince, while Wu Zetian governed the court behind the curtain. Later, Wu Zetian removed Li Xian and became the empress.

Queen Wei (?-710 AD): Born in Shanxi province she was Tang Zhongzong's queen. She was very beautiful when she married, and was highly valued by Tang Zhongzong. However, when Tang

Zhongzong was dying, she committed adultery with Wu Sansi, and promoted the Wei family to powerful positions within the court. When Tang Zhongzong died, Li Longji (Tang Xuanzong) raised an army, stormed the palace, and killed Queen Wei.

Princess Tai Ping (655 AD-713 AD): The youngest daughter of Tang Gaozong and Wu Zetian, and the sister of Tang Zhongzong. She was born in Luoyang, and was greatly loved by her mother Wu Zetian. Her title was Princess Tai Ping. She became powerful in the court, and had a lot of confidants. Li Longji sentenced her to death for conspiracy.

Princess Anle (685 AD-710 AD): Born in Gansu province, she was the daughter of Tang Zhongzong and Queen Wei. Tang Zhongzong had pronounced the Anle princess empress, but many people were against it. Li Longji sentenced her to death.

Princess Changle A fictional character.

Wu Sansi (649 AD-707 AD): Wu Zetian's nephew. When Wu Zetian was the empress, he was entitled King Liang and later became the prime minister. When Tang Zhongzong was in power, his influence was overwhelming. He committed adultery with Queen Wei.

Books:

1. *New book of Tang*, by Song Qi, Ou Yangxiu, Fan Zhen, Lv Xiaqing in Song dynasty.
2. *Old book of Tang*, by Liu Xun.
3. *Old Book of Tang*, volume six, About Wu Zetian.
4. *New Book of Tang*, Volume four, About Wu Zetian.
5. *History Retold as a Mirror for Rules*, The volume of Tang, Wu Zetian Empress.
6. *The Old book of Tang*, volume of Tai Zong.
7. *History Retold as a Mirror For rules*, Volume 199

8. *The New book of Tang, Anle princess.*

9. *The new book of Tang,* volume three.

10. *The old book of Tang,* volume seven, about Tang Zhongzong.

11. *The New book of Tang,* volume four, about Tang Zhongzong.

12. *History Retold as a Mirror for Rules,* on Queen Wei.

13. *Complete Prose Works of the Tang,* on Tai Ping princess

14. *Wu Sansi, the website of ancient China*

Scholarly research:

1. Qiu Luming, *Biography on the Gravestone and Biographies in Historical Writings: Life and Images of Shangguan Wan'er.* China Academic Journal Electronic publishing House.

2. Du Wenyu, *The Talent and Education of Shangguan Wan'er,* 2013, CNKI.

3. *History book of five thousand years of China.* Chapter 20, the history of Tang dynasty.

5. Du Wenyu, *The misreading of Shangguan Wan'er,* China Academic Journal Electronic Publishing House

6. Tai Ping Princess, *Interesting historical stories,* 24, 06, 2015

Internet resources:

Shangguan Wan'er: https://www.gushimi.org/shiren/32.html

Story Three

Three

Zhuo Wenjun of the three risky moves

A portrait of Zhuo Wenjun.

Chapter One

The early years of
Zhuo Wenjun

Unlike the other legendary ladies in this book, Zhuo Wenjun was lucky enough to be born in a time of peace. She was born during the reign of Han Wu (r. 157 BC-87 BC) in the Western Han dynasty (202 BC–9 AD), about 2000 years ago. The emperor succeeded in repelling the invasion of the Hun tribe and had many successful political achievements. The Han dynasty was powerful and enjoyed a high level of prestige in the neighbouring kingdoms.

Starting from Han Wu Emperor's rule, the main religion had changed from Taoism to Confucianism. Generally speaking, Taoism is an animist religion (nature worship) and preaches the idea of being one with nature. The core of Taoist theory was to allow nature to take its course. According to Taoist doctrines, the government should govern the kingdom by non-intervention. However, when Han Wu came to power, the government encouraged the people to adopt Confucianism. Confucian doctrines outlined strict rules for moral standards in the social hierarchy, with children meant obey their parents without fail, wives to obey their husband dutifully, and civilians to obey the emperor wholeheartedly. Gradually, the newly popular doctrine, Confucianism, prevailed.

Emperor Han Wu encouraged his citizens to receive a good education and serve the dynasty, so Confucianism fitted in well for the government's ideals.

Zhuo Wenjun was indeed lucky as her father, Zhuo Wangsong, was the richest businessman in the Western Han dynasty. He was in the iron industry, and the family had worked in it for decades. He had established numerous connections with officials in the royal court and befriended many people from high society. He was ingratiated by his fellow countrymen. His daughter, Zhuo Wenjun, received an excellent education from a young age. She learned to play music, write poetry, and construct well-written prose.

Before Wenjun had even grown up, her parents had already made a match for her to the son from another well-to-do family. The young couple were married when Wenjun reached eighteen years old. However, the wheel of fortune turned, as after only one year of marriage her husband died of disease. Zhuo Wenjun became a widow and returned to her father's home.

From then on, Wenjun would often sit at the window in her room, looking down at the street below to watch the crowds passing by – people with things to do and places to go. But as a lady, social conventions forbade from freely wandering outside. She longed for a partner. She could not help sighing to her maid, Hong Niang, saying, "What an interesting place it is outside. To see all the different people passing by. I wish I could be with them. Instead, I must stay in this chamber, reading or playing music alone to kill time. What bad luck I have! Why was fate so cruel as to take my husband at such a young age? I can't imagine spending the rest of my life like this."

"No, my lady. You will find another man who will love you wholeheartedly."

"I hope so Niang." Wenjun sighed, "When father holds his banquets, he invites people of all sorts to try and make a good match for me. But none are to my taste. The men have no talent or interest in music or poetry. They only care about money. They are shallow, and only want me for father's wealth. I bet most of them have never even read a book."

"I understand My Lady. You want a mate who is a scholar!"

Wenjun blushed for speaking her heart so openly, and so fell into silence. She started to play the Guqin and sang,

Where is the man of my heart?
With whom I fly across the sky!
We can cross the deep ocean, together,
to see beautiful scenery while seasons turn in
their circle!

Wenjun's Guqin was of the best quality available at that time. It was called a Lüqi, a unique and valuable treasure, which only the very wealthy could afford. It was simple in style, with soft outlines. Hers was made of peach wood, of the best quality, and produced a clean sound. When she played, the touching music hung in the air like mist hung in a wintered valley.

Wenjun's long thin fingers played her Guqin whilst she sang. She could not help feeling sentimental.

Being so young, widowhood did not stop her from being romantic. She could not help it, as it is in the blood of all young people. She dreamed that one day she would find someone to grow old with. Wenjun was willing to make sacrifices for love's sake, if that man was worthy. Little did she know…

Sometimes misfortune can suddenly turn into fortune. All that is needed is a little patience.

Sima Xiangru was a tall and handsome man, who displayed great talent. His dress and manners were elegant. He had intelligent eyes that shone when excited. He was a good conversationalist, witty and funny, with many friends. He read widely, but still failed the Imperial exam every time he took it. The Imperial exam was an important milestone for every young educated man in ancient China, as without passing it, options for reasonable employment were limited. The exam was the medium from which talented young people were chosen to enter officialdom and serve the emperor. Unfortunately, many students spent their entire life taking and retaking the exam, unable to pass.

As for Sima Xiangru, the main reason he failed the exam was that he did not take it seriously. His true love was music. He was talented enough to compose music himself, and he was a master Guqin player. This made him think himself better than other people. Yet, it frustrated him to have failed the exam, and he derided himself. Unlike many others who wrote the exam, he came from a poor family, of which we know very little. Because he was poor, and could not get any employment because he kept failing the exam, his life was never easy, and poverty lurked over him always. Yet he still behaved like a gentleman. With few prospects, he took to drinking, roamed the streets forlorn, and begged when he needed the cash.

One dismal afternoon, with only one coin in his pocket, he entered a wine den, wishing to forget his sorrows, even though he had long learnt that the more he drank, the emptier he felt.

Staring at the floor whilst swaying in his seat, he was aroused when someone patted his shoulder. Sitting up, and turning around, he saw the drunken smile of his friend, Li Wangji. Li Wangji was a small-time businessman, but had friends in high places. Li Wangji patted his friend's shoulder again and asked, "Friend, you failed the exam again?"

Xiangru was greatly offended. With hurt pride he shouted, "You know I don't care for Imperial exams. I only care for music!"

"Don't be so angry. I'm serious and concerned for you. I know music is your life. But you must have a plan for the future?"

"No plans… I guess I'm destined to roam the streets until a miracle happens." He joked with his usual humour.

"Who will give charity to a dandy dressed like you?" Li Wangji laughed.

"You can be so annoying!" Xiangru said as he pushed Li Wangji's hand off his shoulder.

"Cheer up friend. Why not go to the brothel to have a little fun?"

"I have no money for that." Xiangru said as he pushed his drink away. He stared at his friend angrily. Li Wangji was quiet for a while then said, "Have you heard that that beauty, Zhuo Wangsong's daughter, has become a widow after just one year of marriage? She still is so young, nineteen I think."

"Really?" Xiangru was interested.

"Have you met her? She's an extraordinary beauty, good at both music and poetry." Li Wangji seemed to hint at something.

"No, I haven't. I don't know much about her."

I get invited to her father's house from time to time to discuss politics, history and philosophy. Zhuo Wangsong is a generous man, always kind to his guests. He is also willing to listen to any advice given to him.

"Is there a painting of her I could see?" Asked Xiangru, showing more interest in this subject than any else he'd heard for months.

"Funny you ask that, because it was only a week ago that a guest asked Zhuo Wangsong for permission to paint his daughter's portrait. Zhuo Wangsong permitted generously. He called Wenjun to come out and meet the guest who was to paint her. When she came out, she did so with a Lüqi Guqin in her hands. She played a tune for us. She is so good it was bewitching. When she had finished, we applauded and cheered so loudly I think it embarrassed her. But she had to keep playing because the artist was painting. Anyway, when she had finished playing and the artist finished had his rough draft, we were free to see what he had done so far. We were all deeply impressed. He had captured her beauty very well. I asked for a print of the painting when I heard her husband had died. I asked for the print with a purpose in mind".

"Oh," said Xiangru, "What purpose?"

With a smile Li Wangji said, "For you my friend. I did it for you." As he said this he scratched around in his bag until he located a particular scroll, which he passed to Xiangru.

Xiangru's mind was running fast as he looked at the painting. Indeed, she was lovely. He knew the Guqin was a special instrument, one that few people understood or could play. Those who were good at the Guqin always seemed to long for a partner with whom they could share the same passion, just as he did. Xiangru's mind was working fast. He felt that this misfortune of widowhood could make the young woman even more romantic. Xiangru foresaw a golden opportunity.

"Would you be able to take me to one of these banquets?" said Xiangru with hope in his voice.

"Of course, I had a feeling that you would ask me." Li Wangji smiled happily for his friend. "In fact, there happens to be one at Zhuo's residence tonight. I may be a drunk, but I am still on the guest register. I will introduce you as a guest. But now you must go to your residence, sober up, clean your clothes, and cleanse your body." Li Wangji blinked his eyes as he upended his cup and gulped down the contents.

ㅋㅋㅋㅋㅋ

Arriving at his tiny hut, Xiangru immediately had a bowl of soup to sober himself up. Then he took a long bath in scented herbs. With care, he put on his best white outfit. With time, and shaking hands, he set about to compose a song. His intention was to play the song this night to whatever audience there was.

He was so engrossed in his task that time passed in the blink of an eye. Finally, the time for the banquet arrived and Xiangru presented himself at the Zhuo residence. Before entering, he took a deep breath.

He found that it was a big event, and that many high-ranking officials were in attendance.

Zhuo Wangsong, aware of his daughter's melancholy and the need to find her another suitor, asked his daughter to make herself up and be prepared to play her Guqin to the audience. He knew that news of the death of her husband would have spread far and wide, and this would bring out all sorts of young bucks to try and win this gem. In fact, this was the main but hidden purpose of tonight's banquet.

Wenjun was reluctant, but her father pushed her into it by saying it would be good for her. She doubted but acquiesced whilst thinking to herself, *father is boring and his friends are boring. There is likely to be no one of interest there.* Yet she still felt an element of excitement, almost like a slight hunch.

ㄱ ㄱ ㄱ ㄱ ㄱ

It was noisy in Zhuo Wangsong's residence, with different groups of people talking and laughing, each group unconsciously competing by raising their voices louder and louder.

Sima Xiangru, sitting with his friend Li Wangji, felt his heart pounding. He scrutinised the guests, trying to spot any potential competition. All the guests were luxuriously dressed. His clothes, although good, were not of the same rich material as theirs. *Would this ambitious plan work?* He wondered as he scanned the room for Zhuo Wenjun.

As he waited, he carried a uniquely dignified air. With his height and bearing, people noticed him.

He listened to the various conversations, and felt as if most were talking nonsense. Xiangru heard one young gentleman comment, "I hope Emperor Han Wu continues enlarging the territory – he must not hold back. We must show our fists to our neighbours!" Xiangru shook his head and said to his friend, "Did you hear that? I detest war and killing. The dynasty should be careful as wars are economically costly, and a waste of soldiers' lives. Living in peace and security, as we are, why should we go out of our way to offend other races?"

Li Wangji nodded whilst Xiangru continued ranting, "The Han Wu emperor has already taught the Hun tribe a lesson. They will be more cautious in their aggression to us. But if we keep prodding them, they will be forced to respond with aggression." "Yet, and it is the common citizens who suffered the most. They, more than anyone, want a peaceful life." said Li Wangji.

They were quiet, until they heard another man bragging, "It was a waste of money to send Zhang Qian to explore the west. He hasn't returned for many years. For all we know he may have been killed, or even have betrayed the Han Dynasty."

"Chicken-minded person!" Xiangru said, rather too loud. "If we do not know the world, how are we going to defend ourselves? If we close our doors, refusing to make friends with our neighbouring countries, we will surely be defeated like a turtle caught in a jar. Moreover, seeking opportunities in the west would increase the government's revenue. We could trade with their merchants for the goods that we have in surplus, and bring back goods we lack. In this way, we would increase the dynasty's wealth."

They lapsed into silence, and Xiangru sank into his own thoughts. He was soon bought back to reality when Zhuo Wangsong, their host, suddenly stood up and raised his cup, "Let's drink, to the prosperity of the Han dynasty!"

"For the prosperity of Han dynasty," they all echoed, lifting their cups to their mouths.

At this time, her face half veiled, Zhuo Wenjun regally entered the room, holding her Lüqi Guqin in her arms. She immediately attracted the attention of the audience. Almost every man in the room was holding his breath, stunned by her stately grace. Despite not being able to see her face clearly, Sima Xiangru was awestruck. The image of Zhuo Wenjun carrying her instrument was too beautiful to be real. For once, he was speechless.

Placing the Guqin on a table, she announced in a soft but clear voice, "I am about to play a 'good night song' to celebrate this happy night."

Wenjun, without looking at the audience, started playing. Her music filled the chamber with a deep resonance. The listeners' imagination played with her. Her gentle fingers played the strings with rhythm and confidence. Xiangru was totally intoxicated. Tears blurred his eyes, and in that moment felt that they were predestined for each other.

When her fingers stilled, the music remained in the chamber, and took some time to dispel. The audience waited for the last sound to evaporate before shouting, "Wonderful!" and the room filled with applause.

Wenjun stood and bowed, then sat and started playing another piece. The effect was just the same. This time, she intended to leave after bowing, but three or four young men rushed to her, as if in a race to reach her first. Xiangru, though, had other plans. He went to the host, and said in a voice that flowed like liquid honey,

"My dear Zhuo Wangsong," as he said this, he made a deep bow, "Your daughter is exquisite, and plays music like an angel... I ... I myself write and play music... and it was just this afternoon that I wrote a song. I would be most honoured to be able to play it for you and your guests."

"Oh, of course!" Zhuo Wangsong uttered with surprise whilst appraising the man in front of him – a gentleman, but not of the same class. His clothes, although smartly pressed, were made of inferior material. Nevertheless, he was always willing to support up-and-coming talent, "What is your name?"

"I am Sima Xiangru," the young man said with confidence.

As Wenjun disengaged herself from the boring suitors, she noticed her father in discussion with a handsome and noble figure. Because he was talking, she had time to observe him. Her intuition suggested that he was different from the men who she met in her daily life. He looked honest, clever and intelligent. What's more, he must have been erudite and of noble character to be able to hold her father in conversation for such a long time.

"Guests, your attention please. Not only have you had the honour to hear my daughter play, but we also now have another young, and I am sure talented, musician. Please welcome Sima Xiangru, he is to..."

Zhuo Wenjun felt her heart somersault, and wondered it if was something she had eaten. She purposely retreated to the next room, leaving her Guqin in the room for the mysterious guest to play. She put an ear to the wall to hear his playing and singing.

When Xiangru saw Wenjun leave the room, he felt disappointed and even a little ashamed of himself for his connivance. But now that he had committed himself, he had no choice but to continue. With complicated feelings, he said, "Good evening, my host, ladies and gentlemen. I will play the Guqin that belongs to the young lady. I hope I do it as much justice with it as she does! I will sing a composition I created only this afternoon. It is entitled *Seeking a female Phoenix mate*. I hope you enjoy it."

Xiangru cleared his throat and sang, softly at first, then louder in order to have the people in the next room hear.

There is but one beauty in the world,
since my first sight of you.
Your image will never be dispelled from my mind.

Zhuo Wenjun's image was deeply embedded into his mind, which gave emotive power to the music.

Not seeing you would drive me insane.
I am like a male phoenix,
seeking my soul mate.
The male phoenix, circulating around the sky,
searching for his love, for you.
Driven by more than instinct,
criss-crossing the heavens.
For you to hear the music that I wrote for you!
Are my words worthy of your love?
Oh, to fly with you
hand in hand,
tonight.
Without you, I have no wings.
Before encountering you,
I knew not where to go.
A beautiful lady, so near, yet far.

Love sickness punishes my heart.

Let's fly high together, shoulder to shoulder.

Each for the other,

are you willing to come to me, tonight?

Let's open our wings... Otherwise...

Otherwise...

There were several verses more, but it only took one for Wenjun to be smitten. Each word stirred her, as if his gentle hands caressed her face. Both enchanted and confused, she leant against the wall for support. Wenjun's face was burning. She had always been romantic, longing to meet the right man to share her life with. But she put that out of her mind when her father committed her to the man who became her husband. She had long acted as the obedient daughter and married the fellow her father had arranged for her. However, fate rendered her a widow. What a twist of fate!

But now, this man appeared from nowhere. *This man, who is he, such a voice, and such musical talent?*

As she kept listening, every word touched her heart. Excitement bubbled up inside her. She knew she was capable of loving deeply. *Does this man hate war, greed and corruption, as I do?*

Her thoughts were interrupted "My lady," it was Hong Niang, "what are you doing leaning against the wall with your eyes closed... Are you sick?"

Wenjun replied by putting her finger to her lips and mouthed "Quiet. Listen."

Worried, Niang stood still and quiet, ready to catch her mistress should she fall.

When the music stopped, with a voice that dripped with emotion Wenjun said "Did you ever hear such music before?"

"Yes. Though I don't understand the music, it sounds touching."

"What do you think of the man who played the music?" Wenjun asked.

The maid peered through the crack of the door, between hinge and wall, herself enjoying the secret, giggled, "He's handsome, and has a nice smile."

"Yes. Yes." Wenjun said as if in a dream, "He does...."

Wenjun pulled Niang close and whispered, "That man's song is meant only for me, he's sending a message to me."

Again, the maid was worried. "Message, what message?"

"He is asking me to elope with him at midnight."

"What?" Niang nearly screamed out of surprise.

"Hush!"

"What are you going to do?"

"I don't know. I have to admit that I have fallen in love with him at first sight. But it is difficult for me to elope with him, because it is against my upbringing as a proper lady."

"My lady, why are you hesitating? Don't you know how romantic it is to elope with a man who you consider to be your soul mate! If I ever encountered such a man, who declared his love so boldly to me in song, I would run away with him without hesitation. Didn't you say just yesterday that you worried that you would always remain a widow?"

The maid's words helped Wenjun make up her mind. Yes, she had a romantic soul. She knew she did not want a man just for his title or wealth. What's more, the man must understand her – music and literature would bind their souls together. She said with excitement to Niang, "You must help me. You must secretly hand him a note. I will tell him... tell him I will meet him at midnight... by the garden, outside?"

Niang nodded her head, her eyes open wide, earnest. Influenced by her lady, she was longing to have a romantic adventure herself.

"Of course, my Lady. I will do as you ask. No one will see me give the note."

ᄀ ᄀ ᄀ ᄀ ᄀ

After Sima Ma Xiangru finished, the room burst into spontaneous applause, as all recognised his musical brilliance. Zhuo Wangsong was delighted as it seemed that he had 'discovered' this genius. He wore a smile from ear to ear.

Sima Xiangru stood up, bowed to the audience, and in a modest tone thanked everyone for their generous applause.

Despite his plain clothes, his breeding was evident. There were many who felt inferior to this young musician, despite their elegant dress. Many of the guests went to pat him on the back and congratulate him. A toast was given, "To young talent!" Zhuo Wangsong asked Xiangru to sit next to him so he could enquire as to his family and career. Xiangru maintained his humour, and answered with dignity and respect but ambiguously to avoid exposing his current situation of living alone and in poverty. His parents died when he was eighteen years old. Since then he made a pittance of a living by copying calligraphy and drawing. Xiangru was a little absent minded as he answered Zhuo Wangsong's questions, as he anxiously wondered if Zhuo Wenjun received his message in the song. And, more importantly, how she was going to respond?

A servant circulated in the banquet room pouring wine for the guests. When she approached Xiangru, she asked, "Wine Master?" and discretely placed her mistress's folded note into his hands. He immediately felt his heart skip a beat. Impatiently, he asked Zhuo Wangsong for permission to go to the washroom. As he crossed the large hall, he was a muddle of happiness and worry.

When he was alone, he opened the note with shaking hands. His heart nearly stropped when he read the beautifully scripted words, *Yes. In the outside garden at midnight.*

He took a deep breath, and became strangely calm. His heart sang the songs of a million birds.

Later, as he left the building, he shouted enthusiastically, "I am happy!" Stunned, people assumed he was drunk. He was a little giddy.

Never in his wildest dreams did he think that a treasure such as Zhuo Wenjun, an educated and beautiful lade from a wealthy a family, would ever consider risking her reputation and give up everything to elope with him.

Suddenly he worried. *How would he look after her? Would she be able to escape the household? What if they were caught by her father? Was she ready for a future, which would start in poverty and shame?* He stopped and stood still. *Oh, my dear, what have I done? I sincerely hope that fate shows mercy on me, to allow me to bring my love back home! After seeing her, my only wish is her happiness. Yet, she agreed.*

There were still three hours before the appointed meeting time. He rushed back to his home to prepare what he could. He kept seeing her in his mind with every minute and hour that passed. At last, Xiangru rode his horse to the meeting place, carrying a man's outfit which he hoped would fit Zhuo Wenjun as a disguise.

At midnight he anxiously waited in the garden and wondered if she would change her mind, or worse, if she would be caught.

爭 爭 爭 爭 爭

Zhuo Wenjun's, mind was in turmoil. Her love for Xiangru was deep; however, she was fully aware that she was gambling with her family fortune. She did not know Xiangru, and had not even spoken to him, but said she yes to elopement! This indeed was a test of her judgement. Was it longing or intuition that told her that he was an extraordinary man? With the time approaching midnight she felt fearful. What if she was wrong? What if the man was just another dandy or a playboy who dressed up as a gentleman? Niang tried to pacify her, "My lady, you always trust your judgement. What's more, you love him, don't you? There is no simpler thing than two people who love each other. Be brave and stay calm, My Lady."

Zhuo Wenjun nodded her head. Yes, if she dare take such a gamble, she must be ready for the consequences. For love, she would risk everything.

With the help of Niang, she packed a few clothes and some jewellery.

As they planned, Niang, who was about the same size as Wenjun, dressed as if she were the young woman with a veil covering her face. From a distance she would pass scrutiny.

Wenjun, in turn, dressed as the servant.

Then, walking together, the maid walked as regally as her maidly body would allow, and Wenjun, slumped as if a tired maid, headed towards the gate. "My Lady Wenjun, where are you going?" One of the guards asked.

Intimating her lady's voice, Niang haughtily replied, "To pick flowers before I sleep."

The guard rebuked, "Master says that ladies are forbidden to go out at night."

Niang pretended to be angry and said, "You are just a guard, how dare you stop me!"

The compromised guard knelt down, "Sorry, my Lady, but we must obey the order from the Master that ladies are not allowed out at night."

"I need the flowers urgently. The aroma of flowers will help me sleep... But if I am not allowed to go out, can my maid pick them for me?"

The guards thought for a while, looked at each other, and said, "It is allowed. Your maid can go out."

The maid, acting as Wenjun said, "Maid, you know the flowers I want. Go and pick them. I shall retire to my bed chamber, hurry."

Wenjun secretly mouthed "Thank you" as she strode out the gate, towards the garden.

Earlier, they discussed the fact that her father would question the maid. *Tell him that you thought we were playing a game on the guards. That it was just for fun. Tell him that you thought I would soon come back with flowers, and we would giggle in delight at the trick. If he asks what I took, say you did not know that I took anything.* She also gave Niang some money in case her father drove her out of the house.

"You can be free if you want."

"Thank you, My Lady."

Wenjun thanked her maid one more time by giving her a sisterly hug, and they headed out of the room.

习 习 习 习 习

Wenjun's heart was beating ferociously as she walked into the darkness. *Is this worth it?* The street was so quiet she could hear her own erratic breath.

Against the wall of the garden, in the shadows, she saw a figure and horse. She headed towards him. When Xiangru saw Wenjun, he had mixed feelings, of love, gratitude, passion, desire, and even deceit. They embraced, and he held her tightly. In the pale light, he took her face in his hands, and whispered, "Thank you."

He helped her into the man's clothes, and onto the horse, and then climbed up behind her. The yellow moon in the dark sky illuminated the way as the horse quickly clip-clopped towards Sima Xiangru's dishevelled home.

Chapter Two

Together in marriage

They had eloped successfully. Perhaps they were even the first successful case of elopement of a well-to-do rich young lady with a poor, penniless man in ancient China.

On the way to Sima Xiangru's home, Wenjun dreamt of a life full of romantic dreams and happiness. However, her dream would soon be broken by cruel reality.

When Wenjun arrived at his shabby house, she was too shocked to speak. The house was covered in dust, with very little furniture; the walls were bare – utterly destitute. The rain, when it came, dripped in through the roof, almost unabated. Even the bed was damp. Sadness overwhelmed her as she was awakened by the splash of cold water in her face. The romantic dream of the shining prince who stole her heart was in fact a poor, plainly dressed man of humble birth. She felt deceived. She beat Xiangru's chest with her small fists, and shouted that he had cheated her. But Xiangru hugged her tightly and gently kissed her. Wenjun stopped beating and leant into him, as a tear descended her cheek. He continued to hold her, smiled and whispered in her ear, "I promise this is not going to last long. Give me a chance."

The next day, things were no better. They needed money to buy food and provisions. Looking at the depressing threadbare room, again, she said, "You deceived me!"

Xiangru maintained his good humour and said mischievously, "Because I love you. Besides, don't you trust your own judgement? I don't believe that you're eloping with me was just an impulse. You must have seen something in me."

Wenjun became silent. Examining her heart knew she loved him, but even so, she shuddered when she looked around their threadbare room.

㵢 㵢 㵢 㵢 㵢

From then on, they lived together. There was no wedding ceremony.

Wenjun was afraid that her beauty would fade in this gloomy poverty. That she would turn into a grumpy and bad tempered hag. She worried that she would have nothing interesting to talk about.

Xiangru said he had to go out on an errand. When he returned, Wenjun realised that he had sold the elegant clothes he had worn last night to buy food. Depressed, she said nothing, went to the kitchen, lit a fire, and cooked the food he had purchased – it was the first time in her life that she had cooked.

Wenjun hoped such days of poverty would not last. Without money, they could barely feed themselves and often bickered. Both became frustrated; love was not what she had imagined.

She decided to ask for her father's forgiveness, and to persuade him to accept Xiangru as her husband.

When Xiangru and Wenjun arrived at Zhuo Wangsun's gate, the guard stopped them from entering.

"I am your lady, don't you recognise me?" Wenjun said with dignity.

"Yes, but Master has said that you are never to enter this house."

"Why? Father, father!" Wenjun shouted hysterically with a sore heart. She was praying that her father's cold heart would be warmed.

"Master has given us clear orders. You are forbidden to enter. There is no use shouting. Don't blame us for being rude."

Xiangru wrapped his arms around Wenjun to stop her from shouting. He whispered gently in her ear, "There is no need to shout like this. We must return home." Xiangru was conscious of the pain in his heart. Wenjun's face was covered in dusty tears. Xiangru, with a smile, wiped the tears from her face and said, "Don't worry. It will be fine. Let's go."

He helped Wenjun onto the horse and they went away as fast as they could. Xiangru was angry. Loving her, he should have left her alone to live her life of privilege. Now she lived a poor life with him, because of her love for him. By what right could he rob her of her father's love?

Chapter Three

Sima Xiangru climbs into the saddle

Zhuo Wangsong complained to his entire circle of friends and business associates about his ungrateful daughter. The girl was disinherited as she had brought shame to the family. If she dared to return and ask for mercy, he would drive her out of the door as if she were a dog.

What was strange, though, was that Wenjun's faithful maid was not punished by Zhuo Wangsong. It would seem that the answers they had prepared satisfied the Master that she was not an accomplice. She continued working in Zhuo Wangsong's household.

The harsh words of Zhuo Wangsong spread quickly to Wenjun and Xiangru's ears. It saddened them both, but Wenjun was pleased her faithful maid had not suffered. Xiangru endeavoured to earn enough money to support them both.

ㅋ ㅋ ㅋ ㅋ ㅋ ㅋ

Time passed slowly, and every time Wenjun thought of her hard-headed father, she could not help but cry. She had sold most of the precious items that she had taken with her. She loved Xiangru even more and did not regret the decision she made on the night of the banquet, despite their poverty. On most nights, she found it hard to fall asleep. In these moments she tried to figure out a way to get out of poverty. One morning whilst still in bed, Wenjun rolled towards her husband, "Why don't we open a wine bar in the town centre to make money?" Xiangru felt a pang of sadness at his futility. He had tried to get commissions writing and translating, but all doors were closed to him. He covered his face with his hands and wept.

Wenjun smiled faintly. She had made the right choice once, and was sure she was doing so again.

Wenjun sold the last of her jewellery and Xiangru sold their horse. With this small amount of money, they opened a bar in a back street of the town.

The news that Zhuo Wangsong's daughter had become a barmaid and lived in the slum with her pathetic husband spread through the town like wildfire. People felt sorry for the princess who had turned into a sparrow because of love.

But secretly, many admired her for her bravery to pursue love for love's sake. She was the most talked about topic in the city. People came from all over town to buy a drink in the wine bar, just out of curiosity, to see the flower that now grew in the dung heap.

Wenjun bore this curiosity with the eye of a business woman. She did not show anxiety on her face and treated every guest with humility and hospitality, whilst graciously accepting their money. She answered their curious questions unreservedly. This only added to people's respect for her.

She still hoped to win back her father's favour, but if not, so be it. Xiangru did his bit, and ran to and fro in the now busy bar. Wenjun stood at the counter, and observed Xiangru busily and with good nature welcome the customers. In her wildest dreams she never imagined becoming a barmaid in order to survive. She knew she was happy at the moment with Xiangru, however, she did not know how long a love set in poverty would last.

In the evening, after the bar closed, they often looked at the sky and marvelled at the stars. Xiangru hugged Wenjun, and said, "I have made up a story for you."

"Really? Tell me."

"The title is *The Praise of a Beauty*.

Listen to me. Sima Xiangru, a very handsome man from the Liang Kingdom (a fictional kingdom made up by Xiangru), *just returned from his mission to the Wu Kingdom for peace negotiations. An intimate official of the King of Liang had slandered Sima Xiangru by whispering in the king's ear, 'My dear lord, Xiangru is too ambitious. He has enchanted you with sweet words to get close to your concubines!'*

The King of Liang asked Sima Xiangru in turn, "Do you love beautiful women?" Sima Xiangru said honestly, "No! Not a bit."

The King asked, "You don't love beauty, can you compare yourself with Mo Tzu, or Confucius?" Xiangru shook his head and said, "Confucius once ran away from a beauty without even seeing what she looked like. Mo Tzu behaved in the same way to avoid having contact with any beauty. This can only prove that both Confucius and Mo Tzu were scared of beautiful women. If they never saw beautiful lady, how could they claim that they did not love them? This is not the case for me, the only person in this world who holds my attention is Wenjun, even with beauties sitting on my lap.

"I can tell you another story about my acquaintance of a beauty.

"When I was young, I lived alone on the west side of the kingdom. I had an empty house. There was a lady who lived near me. She was so beautiful, with a pair of bright eyes, thick cloudy hair, and a glorious smile. She always looked forward to meeting me, for me to come to her room. But I pretended not to know her heart. The lady was disappointed, until she married another man many years later.

"Your majesty, I admire your open mindedness. You are surrounded by all the beauties of the world. However, I dared not, nor have any interest to cast an eye on them, for I already have a beauty. One who sleeps with me every night? I had already taken her as my wife. Do you know how I met her? One day, I heard someone playing the Guqin, so I opened the door, and found an earthly paradise in an exquisitely decorated room. I saw an angel in front of me. She told me that she lived alone, and she asked, 'Which Kingdom do you come from?' I said, 'I am from Liang Kingdom.' So the angel made a toast with me, and invited me to play music for her. I played music to praise her beauty. I sang as I played, and the beauty left for the next room. My heart was broken whenever I thought of her departure. I wondered whether the lady would dare to become engaged to me without the permission of her father. Since then, I cast no eyes on other beauties.

"That's why I said Confucius and Mo Tzu were inferior to me when resisting temptation from the charm of a beauty."

Wenjun laughed merrily when she heard the story. Obviously, Xiangru was making fun of her. However, under her joyful happiness lay a deep anxiety and emptiness in her mind. Though currently they were happy, what if they were one day turned out on the street, without a roof over their head – this poverty was a serious problem. Wenjun was aware that their happiness could be a flash in the pan. They had to eat and get furniture. By wasting their talent in the bar, resentment could creep in. What was worse, she, as a lady of high rank, was falling into mediocrity. Life would change her into an old woman. Wenjun smiled a painful smile, "You are so talented, why do you prefer to waste your talent to compose such love prose to tease me? You should rather devote yourself to studying the classics and literature, pass the Imperial examination and gain position. If you could prove your value, father would forgive us!"

Xiangru grumbled for a while, but said reluctantly, "I promise I will never make you suffer. I will make you the happiest woman in this world."

Wenjun prayed secretly in her heart. She trusted him, but would that day come soon?

習 習 習 習 習

Zhuo Wangsong constantly thought of his daughter, but never allowed her name to be mentioned. He became morose, quickly losing his temper. He wanted to forgive her but could not. He felt betrayed. Why would she elope with Sima Xiangru without informing him, and ruin her precious reputation? *I would have given her to him if she asked.* For a young educated lady, she could have been with any eligible young man of high rank, but instead she chose a pauper. He was wondering whether her education had just been a waste of his money! Wenjun's elopement changed Zhuo Wangsong. He was no longer a happy and generous old man. Gone were the banquets, as he submerged into deep sorrow.

At this moment, his old acquaintance Li Wangji came to visit him. He had always planned to be the matchmaker between his friend Xiangru and Zhuo Wenjun. He was somewhat relieved when he was bought in by the servant. Zhuo Wangsong, in bad temper grouched, "I have always treated you as a friend, why did you bring a wolf into my house! You brought misfortune on to my family!"

Li Wangji paused, waiting for Zhuo Wangsong's anger to relent. He said, "I didn't come to quarrel with you. Besides, what is done cannot be undone. I came to bring news of your daughter. I want you to understand."

"Understand what?"

"Your daughter and Xiangru really love each other. Through necessity they have opened that wine bar. Your dearest daughter has fallen into the lowest rank of people and she is the talk of the town. You daughter has committed no crime, other than to fall love with a man who is of lower rank."

Zhuo Wangsong closed his eyes and sighed, "I had no choice but to disown her."

"You do not lack money. Why not show kindness towards your daughter and accept your son-in-law? I know Sima Xiangru is an upright man, noble, erudite and generous of spirit. With support, one day, he is sure to become a successful person. It's just a matter of time. You heard his music, his lyrics. You spoke to him, and you were even pleased that you had 'discovered' him".

Zhuo Wangsong said, "I'm too old for this. I hate the thought of my daughter making a fool of herself and the family. I miss my daughter… Perhaps you can do me a favour by taking a message to my son-in-law that I will give them a small allowance. Also see that she gets her Guqin to play. I will support them, but she must stop selling wine and bringing shame to my family!"

Wenjun was astonished by the sudden change of generosity of her father, and smiled in gratitude as Li Wangji gave her her beloved Guqin. Wenjun caressed her beautiful Guqin, and started to play *Seeking a female Phoenix mate*, the composition her husband created. Sadness swirled in her mind. Xiangru listened and also become emotional.

Wenjun played music all afternoon, and the strain of the last few years emerged in the music. Suddenly, there was a disharmonious sound as a string broke.

It was at that moment he made an oath to himself and to her. He did not want his beloved wife to ever suffer again because of his inadequacy. He must stand up on his own two feet. From that moment on, he devoted himself to studying literature and classical books. With his wife's help, he would pass the Imperial exam.

His studies brought them closer together as they often discussed political issues until late at night. They composed poetry, prose, and even couplets together. For the first time since they married, they were having fun.

Xiangru could not forget how Wenjun suffered for his sake, and so was determined. It was imperative that he make a name for himself. He wanted to make her happy. It was the first time in his life that Xiangru was doing something for another person. All too soon, the date of the Imperial exam arrived.

The results were released. A messenger came to the couple's home and announced the good news that Xiangru had gained first place out of all the candidates.

为 为 为 为 为 为

It was by coincidence that the emperor, Han Wu, ended up reading Xiangru's fictitious and amusing story. It was titled *Zi Xu's Narration:*

"The emperor of the Kingdom of Wu asked Zi Xu to be the ambassador to Kingdom of Qi.

The emperor of the Kingdom of Qi had taken an entire military troop for a hunt he was on, and invited Zi Xu to accompany him. When the hunt was over, Wu You from the Kingdom of Qi asked Zi Xu his impression of the hunt with emperor of Qi. Instead of saying something diplomatic, Zi Xu belittled the Qi Kingdom by saying how wonderful the Wu Kingdom was. He gave three examples: the food, the landscape, and the lovely ladies in the Kingdom of Wu.

Wu You laughed at Zi Xu for his shallowness. He argued back. Firstly, King Qi deployed an entire troop on the hunt, not to show off, but out of respect towards Kingdom of Wu. Secondly, Zi Xu must have exaggerated the magnificence of the Kingdom of Wu by using impossible examples. If what he described was real in the Kingdom of Wu, then the emperor of Wu must be a foolish emperor, who ignored his political work. If the reality was not like what he described, it only proved that Zi Xu himself was a liar."

Emperor Han Wu was amused by the story and burst out laughing. He was impressed by Xiangru's beautiful phrases and convincing argument. Most of all, there was an irony and humour in his composition that most people lacked.

From this impression, the Han Wu Emperor thought Xiangru would make a good official as he was clever and clear thinking. He would start as a junior advisor. The Han Wu Emperor announced, "Sima Xiangru was the number one scholar in this year's Imperial examination, and he will be coming to the capital."

The emperor sent escorts to bring his official invitation to Xiangru. This news spread fast and reached Zhuo Wangsong's ears in no time. He was greatly relieved. At last! Ever since the scandal of his daughter's secret engagement with Xiangru, Zhuo Wangsong had felt humiliated. Now, finally, his daughter and her husband had gained face in the community. It proved that his dear daughter was farsighted enough to choose a good husband for herself. She could judge a person with her good sense, and saw that Xiangru was the hidden gem among the common people. Her education was not a waste of time. It worked! It worked! Nobody cared where heroes came from. Finally, Zhuo Wangsong laughed. He was himself again. He also accepted their marriage, even though there was no actual ceremony, saying, "The rice is already cooked, there is no uncooking it."

In fact, to celebrate Xiangru's first place in the Imperial exam, and Xiangru's rise to prominence, Zhuo Wangsong decided to hold a banquet at his residence. He proudly welcomed his daughter and son-in-law as special guests. Xiangru gladly accepted the invitation on their behalf.

"Congratulations!" said Zhuo Wangsong to his son-in-law, with kindness yet with authority in his voice.

"Thank you, my dear father. It is late, but I thank you for allowing me to marry your precious daughter. Wenjun is the most valuable treasure in my life." He said this with a rascal's smile, but was still full of respect. He was good at making people feel comfortable. He personally served his father-in-law tea, and even gently massaged Zhuo Wangsong's painful back. He took a moment while doing the massage to say, "Sorry, father. I stole your daughter without your permission. I now know I was wrong to do that, but I promise that I will never make her unhappy. Thank you for your kindness and forgiveness."

"Good, well done, my boy." said Zhuo Wangsong with a genuine smile. "I am glad that you have admitted your mistakes. People are not perfect. They always make one mistake or another, big or small. Luckily, you are a good boy, active and progressive. You finally washed my daughter's shame away with your achievement, and proved she is farsighted. Ha-ha-ha."

Zhuo Wangsong was relaxed by Xiangru's massage, his eyes closed and his mood was good. "The reason why I have asked the whole family to come to the banquet is to announce that you and my daughter are a part of our family, tied to us by blood." He then turned to his daughter who was smiling, intoxicated with happiness and relief. Zhuo Wangsong shrugged his shoulders, and said, "Sorry, my dear daughter. I have wronged you. I thought you had run away with a rascal, but this boy proved that he is worthy of your love and our family's support. In order to support you both, I have decided to share half of my fortune with you and Xiangru. The other half will go to my younger son!"

Both Wenjun and her husband knelt down, kowtowed, and thanked their father wholeheartedly. The atmosphere at this moment was harmonious and respectful. When Zhuo Wangsong recalled this pleasant memory, at an old age, this family banquet was one of his happiest memories.

Wenjun met her faithful maid, Niang, once again in her father's house. Niang was eager to learn if her lady was living well. Wenjun clutched Niang's hands warmly in hers, "Thank you for what you did for us. Although, it was difficult, it turns out he is indeed the right man for me."

"I'm glad my lady, as long as you are happy," Niang said excitedly. Wenjun felt touched. She wiped her tears, and removed a beautiful piece of jade that she always wore, and gave it to her maid as a gift.

ㄱㄱㄱㄱㄱ

Zhuo Wangsong, proud and in high spirits, sent his son-in-law off to the capital city of Chang'an. Crowds of commoners and gentry gathered along the two sides of the road in order to wish the now famous scholar well. Xiangru rode a horse waving at the crowd; he could not help feeling proud and giddy.

Wenjun remained behind in their home. Xiangru had promised to return every few months.

ㄱㄱㄱㄱㄱ

A year passed, but Xiangru did not return home. For Wenjun, time dragged.

Zhuo Wangsong visited his daughter every now and then, asking her if Xiangru had visited. Wenjun felt embarrassed. She struggled to remain cheerful, and at first lied to her father, telling him that Xiangru wrote daily. Zhuo Wangsong was content with his daughter's answer. Wenjun felt uneasy. He was just like mist, here one day, and then gone. Wenjun trusted Xiangru, and so she kept waiting for year after year, until the fifth year. During this time, she often visited her father's residence. Her father shared her worries, but was reassured by his daughter's belief that Xiangru was firm in his love. Afraid to add more worries to his daughter, Zhuo Wangsong avoided raising the topic of Xiangru, and tried to cheer her up.

As time passed, Wenjun felt she was aging. At the age of twenty-five, she felt as if she had been widowed once again, waiting for an impossible husband to return.

Whenever she heard footsteps she would look outside to see if it was him. But it never was. Still, she waited, looking forward for his return, but she received no news, not even a letter. There was some news from the capital that Xiangru had become a close advisor to the emperor and was a busy and important man. They also said he was gaining fame as a writer and scholar.

By the fifth year, there was still no news. Wenjun felt old and awkward. She thought her husband must have lost interest in her. Her bitter tears turned to rage. Was she wrong? Was Xiangru a faithless person? Her indignation and loneliness was such that even her Guqin gave her little comfort. *What should I do?* She had once made one risky move to elope with her husband at the cost of losing everything — her reputation, her money, her youth — with the hope that he was a loyal man. When she closed her eyes, images of Xiangru floated in her mind, enjoying a seductive and lavish time in Chang'an and being chased by a stream of women. She sweated all over. What a heartbreaker! Wenjun swore. When she did play Guqin again, sad music echoed throughout the house. All in the neighbourhood heard the music and wondered why the player was so sad. She was tired of waiting for him in vain day by day, and her tense hand broke one of the strings. She had to do something to win her husband back. The reason why she was silent and did not contact Xiangru was because she felt it was his duty as her husband to write to her first. As he seemed to have forgotten her, she would win his love by taking another risky move.

Wenjun thought as she listened to the rain outside, beating against the windows. Though her life looked ideal to others, she felt its bitter taste.

I made so many sacrifices for him, Wenjun thought to herself bitterly. She needed to speak out, to take action, to rebuke her husband, and win his love back. She called for a messenger. "I want you to deliver a letter to Sima Xiangru in the capital."

"Yes, my lady."

Wenjun thought for a while and wrote thirteen numbers with a half mocking smile on the paper: *one, two, three, four, five, six, seven, eight, nine, ten, one hundred, one thousand, and ten thousand.*

The messenger was confused as he watched Zhuo Wenjun write out these thirteen numbers. He was still waiting and half kneeling down, but seeing that she seemed to have finished, said, "My Lady, is there nothing more you wish to say?"

"No. That's all."

She folded the paper, sealed it, and gave it to the messenger. Before the messenger left, she called him back to instruct him, "Be sure to give the message to him directly. Not to anyone else!"

The messenger was confused, but nodded his head.

기 기 기 기 기

Sima Xiangru was entranced with the golden city of Chang'an. So gorgeous were the buildings, so much to experience. He was thrilled. At the same time, the emperor kept him busy day and night. Han Wu appreciated him for his advice and conversation. The other officers flattered him in order to gain his friendship. Everyone liked Xiangru, and many officials invited him to dinner, either to talk politics or to strengthen their mutual relations. Xiangru was careful and cautious to serve the emperor by taking care of him devotedly, and in this way he quickly won the trust of the emperor. Xiangru would enlighten the emperor by using examples, rather than retorting with provocative language. The Han Wu emperor was always glad to hear Xiangru's anecdotes. Of course, as a sage emperor, he knew the character of all his court officials, so he was aware of the cunning side of Xiangru's character. At one point, Xiangru was appointed as ambassador to negotiate with a foreign tribe to the southwest of the Han dynasty. Xiangru used the carrot and stick method to make those people submit their tribute to the Han emperor. With his continuous effort, the Han Wu Emperor established good relations with neighbouring ethnic groups, and won the peace at the kingdom's borders. Xiangru was greatly rewarded for his success in his political career.

The emperor enjoyed amusement, and there were always many dancers and singers around. He encouraged Xiangru to select any that he desired. Though Xiangru did not marry them as concubines, such a life quickly weakened his will. He took one for one night every now and then.

It was never the intention of Xiangru to be unfaithful or to ignore his wife, but over the years, his memory of her faded. That was until he received the message. The unopened letter bought back memories of her. He felt ashamed of himself. For five years, he had never once asked for leave from Han Wu Emperor so that he could return home and see his wife. He could not imagine how Wenjun endured such loneliness without her husband for five years. He trusted her virtue, but his will was weak.

He opened the letter, expecting a letter full of blame and lovesickness but was astonished to see that there were just weird numbers.

One, ... ten thousand.

What did it mean?

Xiangru was confused. Why did Wenjun not say anything in words? This thought troubled Xiangru. He could neither sit nor stand nor concentrate on anything.

Xiangru felt his wife had outsmarted him. He racked his brains to solve the riddle, but could not. This riddle troubled him so much that he could no longer sleep. Out of worry, he left his bed and stood by the window, hoping a solution would come to him. He did not even notice the half-moon that hung just above the trees.

It was soon to be the Mid-Autumn Festival, a time when families came together to celebrate. Would his wife want him to come home?

He hurriedly wrote back, *Wenjun, my dear wife, how are you? What kind of riddle have you sent to me? I rack my brains but cannot fathom its meaning. Sorry for not writing to you all these years. It is truly unforgivable. I always have you in my mind, but I am so busy. I always remember our marriage oath.*

Yours, in love, Sima Xiangru.

Wenjun finally got the letter from Xiangru. Her hands were trembling, afraid to open it. But with determination she opened the letter. She smiled at last. Such men could only be won through wisdom. Her second chess move was correct. However, she still could not help feeling sad. With indignation, she replied,

You asked me what these numbers mean, so I will tell you.

One: Parting with you for the first time in our life.

Two: Times heaven and earth were turned upside down.

Three and four: You promised that you would return every three or four months.

Five and Six: Nearly six years you have ignored me.

Seven: I'm listless, and have no mood to touch the seven strings of my Guqin.

Eight: Even if you ask me to write a love letter in eight lines, you will not answer.

Nine: The nine ring puzzle that cannot be solved by men, just as my missing you is like a puzzle in my mind.

Ten: The ten thousand miles between us makes me gaze towards you, anxiously, until my eyes are strained, but still, I cannot see your face.

One hundred: I figure out one hundred puzzles in my mind.

One thousand: My worries are just like a thousand entangled silk threads.

Ten thousand: I complain, I have experienced ten thousand days of hardship since the day that I first met you.

I lean on the fence looking for you, gazing far away with an uneasy mind.

Each year when the Chong Yang Festival arrives and families are together, I watched the lonely goose pass by in the sky.

During the Mid-Autumn Festival, when the moon is full and round, you are not by my side.

In July, I burn incense to ask the ancestors, where are you?

In the hottest days in June, everyone fanned to cool themselves, but it only made me sadder.

In May, the pomegranate trees were red, as if touched by blood, but a shower of heavy rain made the petals fall to the ground.

In April, the loquat fruit was still not ready.

I watch myself in the mirror, growing old.

The March peach petals fell on the river, floating away.

In February, the string that was tied to the kite broke in my hands.

Alas, alas, since you left me, I eat without knowing the taste of the food; I have no mood to make up my hair.

Music, chess, painting, and calligraphy hold no interest for me. Day and night I pray for your return.

After the spring is summer,
autumn comes after winter.
My words express my heartbreak.
Every word is written with my blood.

> *There are no words adequate to express my sadness,*
>
> *my grievance and resentment.*
>
> *I shed angry tears.*
>
> *Love-sickness is burning in my mind.*
>
> *I summon all my turbulent feelings in one sentence.*

If there is an afterlife, I want us to be reincarnated me as a man and you as a woman, so you can taste what it is like for a woman to wait in loneliness.

Xiangru was shocked by his wife's narration. His mind was choked with complicated feelings. He thought of the days when he and Wenjun had endured hardship and sold wine together in their bar. Wenjun, a high-ranking lady, had made so many sacrifices for his sake. How could he be so ungrateful and forgetful? What a fool he was! Suddenly, Xiangru's old self reawakened. He immediately went to speak to the emperor.

"My Lord, I have a request."

"What is it?"

"I have a wife in my hometown, with whom I have parted for nearly six years. I never asked for permission to leave my office to visit her. I feel it is shameful for a man to abandon his first wife at home, while he himself enjoys the pleasures in the Golden City. I, as one of your advisors, am setting a bad example to the other officials. I would like permission to bring my wife to Chang'an to live with me."

"Oh, yes, your wife. What is her name again?" The emperor asked in surprise.

"Her name is Zhuo Wenjun."

"Of course, the daughter of Zhuo Wangsong, the businessman?"

"Yes, she is."

"I now remember the love story between you. It has already become legend. What a woman! When she married you, you didn't have a penny in your pocket. What a bold choice she made! If you did not pass the examination and become the number one scholar, you would not have spent a good life together, but rather lived together in poverty and misery.

"Yes, bring her. Let her enjoy life with you here in this city."

"Thank you, my dear Majesty."

The Emperor's words only made Xiangru feel deeper shame. He could not wait to see his wife again.

Wenjun waited for Xiangru's response. She looked at herself in the mirror, feeling that her love sickness had made her thin, her once smooth complexion a withered flower. No message arrived. Had he forgotten about her completely? Or did he have another woman? In deep anguish, Wenjun threw the mirror against the wall, just missing Xiangru as he entered. "What a temper!" he said, grinning.

Wenjun saw the face that haunted her day and night standing in front of her. She saw his expensive clothes, looking tall, strong and handsome. Her man, here.

At first she gasped in happy surprise, but then restrained herself, and said with control and mockery in her eyes, "Why did you bother to return?"

"Because one, two three, four, five, six, seven, eight, nine, ten, one hundred, one thousand… and ten thousand. The same feeling has tortured me day and night."

"Is that right?" Wenjun smiled and started to make herself up in front of the mirror, as if she had not a care in the world. She ignored Xiangru, who was standing there self-consciously, wondering what to say. He finely said, "I want you to return with me to the capital… to live."

Wenjun looked at him, "Do you? Do you still think I am pretty?"

This was the first time that he was able to observe her closely. To his concern, his wife looked wan and shallow, though she used much rouge on her face.

"You are as beautiful as ever," he said with an ache in his heart. He knew it was his absence that had aged her like this.

Wenjun smiled and said easily, "I know you are lying."

Chapter Four

The Song of White Hair

Wenjun and Xiangru said goodbye to Zhuo Wangsong, and left for the capital. Zhuo Wangsong was happy to see his son-in-law return to collect Wenjun. Man and wife should not be apart for so long.

In the city of Chang'an, Xiangru he kept chattering nervously without stopping. Wenjun frowned as she observed everything they passed. In her opinion, Chang'an's prosperity was mixed – there were rich people strutting around the streets or sitting in the most gorgeous carriages, while the poor people lived in slums, begging for food day and night. She gave a few coins to some homeless children that she met on the street.

To be honest, Chang'an was not totally unfamiliar to her as her father had taken her to the city several times when she was young. It was familiar and strange at the same time. She knew that Xiangru kept talking because he was nervous of an awkward silence developing. Wenjun laughed, and said jeeringly, "To be honest, I am already familiar with this place as I have been here with my father. There is no need to introduce the city to me."

Xiangru's face reddened in embarrassment. His wife's joke made him uneasy. He had to treat Wenjun with a respect. He made an extended bow, and said, "My dear, would you like to go home now?"

He held out his hands to Wenjun, who stretched out her hands to take his.

When at his — and now her — home, and settled, she asked, "Tell me about your career. You must be so important if you couldn't even find the time to write me a single letter." She said this with a knitted brow and an ironic tone.

Her question made him flustered, "Yes, my life is busy." Yet, he could not remember what filled his time. It had all just passed by in the blink of an eye. He said with a sigh, "The emperor demands my company. You know about boring politics, everyone telling lies, for better or for worse. In this peaceful time, the sage Emperor Han Wu likes to decide everything himself, unwilling to hear too many contrary opinions. I just support him as best as I can. Sometimes I just talk with him for fun and enlighten him with amusing stories."

"You are good at making up stories. You have been since the first time I met you." Wenjun said with the same irony.

"An official career can sometimes be dangerous. Serving the emperor is most dangerous. Being a sage emperor, he must balance the good and the evil in his mind, and never allow one side to grow stronger than the other. He always has a mirror set in his mind to judge right from wrong. We were not born in a troubled time, with the flames of war engulfing the city. So there is no point remonstrating in court seriously. The safest way to treat an emperor in peaceful times is to enlighten him, and make him calm and easy. Proper advice always needs a good story to embellish it."

Zhuo Wenjun made no comments on this and asked instead, "And women?"

He hesitated, uncomfortable, before saying, "I don't want to lie to you. I have had several women. But each was just for one night."

Wenjun said nothing, and asked flatly, "Do you want to have a concubine?"

"If you will allow me." Xiangru said earnestly. He was nervous, as he fallen for a young and pretty dancing girl, whose name was Bao Chai.

"Oh, you ask me for my permission?" Wenjun said, still with a smile on her face, like a cat playing with a mouse.

"Yes."

"What's she like?"

"She has a pair of eyes as bright as stars, her breast are as two apples. She has a very slender waist, and walks as if she glides on water."

"She is an extraordinary beauty then, is she?"

"Yes, she is."

"And brains? Or don't they matter? Do you want other concubines?"

"I don't know." Xiangru felt cornered by his wife's questions. She did not show any sign of anger, and asked the questions as if she was asking for a cup of tea. Her lack of concern scared him.

"I will give you my answer in the morning." Again, she smiled.

When Xiangru suggested that she sleep by his side, Wenjun refused saying, "I would rather be alone."

ㅋㅋㅋㅋㅋ

The moment Wenjun left the room, her courage collapsed. She was crestfallen. Unnoticed tears dribbled down her cheek.

What a heartbreaker! I have misjudged him. I would rather separate from him with pride than share my husband with another woman. Aaarrrgh! I will break the chains that hang around my neck and leave him! This was the voice whispering clearly in Wenjun's mind. *Why are men so changeable! As soon as he gained glory and achievement, he forgot his first wife, who sacrificed everything for* the sake of love and overcame many hardships with him when the whole world closed their doors to him. Such a heartless, faithless man! All my life, I only wanted one man to cherish me wholeheartedly, to grow old with. I loved him, and he also loved me.

She picked up a bamboo brush and started to write.

The Song of White Hair by Zhuo Wenjun:

In a few short years,

my hair turned white.

Love should be as white mountain snow,

as brilliant as moonlight in the night.

If you give your love to another,

I say goodbye to you, forever.

This is the last time we take a drink together.

Tomorrow, I depart, along the side of the river.

Walking slowly.

Our past beautiful days left behind,

Do you remember them?

Today's departure

is as decisive as the day I eloped with you,

I will not cry sadly, as if a young girl.

For my whole life,

I expected to marry a single-hearted man,

who would never part from me, even when my hair turned white.

True love between men and women should be as a long and soft as a bamboo pole,

as lovely and vivid as fish in the water.

Men should value true love whole heartedly,

there is no remedy for the loss of love,

it can't be bought with mountains of gold, as you are

a three foot tall man!

Leaving the message on the table, Wenjun fell into a restless sleep. The next morning, when the first twilight shone through the window, she quietly opened the door and left the big empty house. Her footsteps were soft and silent.

As she wrote in the message, she would walk slowly along the river's edge, not shedding a single tear, willing herself to leave her past behind. She did not regret any of her choices. Since she was a young girl, she had decided what she wanted in life; and that was to have a man who would not change in love, and love her whole-heartedly forever. If Xiangru was not such a man, she was willing to leave him just as easily as the very day that she decided to elope with him.

The further she went the stronger her determination. She would never allow a man to break her!

It was then that she heard the fast galloping of a horse coming up from behind her. A partial smile formed on her lips. She did not look back, and kept her slow footsteps moving forward. The horse stopped by her side, and she heard a man drop to the ground.

The man encircled his arms around her from behind, grasping her tightly, and said, "Wenjun, I only love you. There will be no others."

"How can I believe you?"

"The moment I read the note, I almost went mad and panicked that I had lost you. I felt as if I was a lost soul. I cursed the servant who claimed he did not to see you go out."

"What if you couldn't find me?"

"I would resign from my office and look for you everywhere until I did."

Wenjun leant happily in his arms and asked, "Are you sure?"

"Yes. I only ever wanted you for love." Xiangru hugged her tightly and whispered in her ear. Wenjun felt relief. She was right again. She had won her love back.

"Will you return home with me?"

Wenjun nodded her head. Xiangru helped her on the horse. He began to sing a beautiful song and she joined in. The song was the one he had composed the night they eloped together, *Seeking a female Phoenix mate…*

Biographies:

Zhuo Wenjun (fl. 2nd century BC): Born in Chengdu during the Western Han dynasty. Her father, Zhuo Wangsong, was the richest businessman in the Western Han dynasty. He traded in iron.

Zhuo Wenjun was beautiful and talented at music and poetry. She eloped with Sima Xiangru after seeing him at a banquet. They lived in poverty for two years. She sold her few valuables to start a wine bar so they could make a living. Later, Sima Xiangru became the number one scholar Imperial scholar in the land, proving that she had made a wise choice.

Sima Xiangru (c. 179-117 BC): Born in Chengdu. He was a famous writer who lived during the Western Han dynasty. Born to a very poor family, he was nonetheless a talented young man. During a banquet organised by Zhuo Wangsong, he played a piece of self-composed Guqin music titled *Seeking a female Phoenix mate*, which immediately won Zhuo Wenjun's heart. She eloped with him.

After coming first in the Imperial examination, he moved to Chang'an to serve the emperor. He wrote many famous poems and prose, including *Zi Xu's narration* and *Praise of beauty*. He was greatly honoured by the Han Wu Emperor. Later, at the age of sixty he resigned from his office because of illness.

Zhuo Wangsong: Born in Sichuan province. He was extremely rich due to his successful trade in iron. He was the richest business person in the Western Han dynasty, just below the Han Wu Emperor.

Han Wu Emperor (157–87 BC): The seventh emperor of Western Han dynasty. He loved literature and was good at composing prose.

His political achievements include establishing the foreign court system, the governor system, the judicial system, and strengthening the monarchy and centralisation. The government monopolised the operation of the salt, iron, and wine industries, and restrained the power of wealthy merchants.

In terms of culture, he abolished *Hundred schools of thought* and promoted Confucianism.

In foreign affairs, Emperor Wu adopted a policy of expansion. He had fought a prolonged war against Hun. He assigned some officials to explore the western regions, and started the trading route along the Silk Road. However, later under his governance, the kingdom's treasury was greatly drained by continuous war. He died at the age of seventy.

Books:

Historical records, the story of Sima Xiangru, by Sima Qian

History of Han dynasty, About Sima Xiangru, by Ban Gu.

Scholarly research:

Liu Haibing, *The clever home letter of Zhuo Wenjun,* from common literature book.

Wen Hong Xia, *The Three risky chess moves of Zhuo Wenjun,* China Academic Journal Electronic Publishing House.

Bai Liang, *Sima Xiangru, and Zhuo Wenjun, the earliest eloping couple,* China Academic Journal Electronic Publishing House.

Internet Sources:

A complete collection of Zhuo Wenjun's Poetry https://so.gushiwen.org/authors/authorvsw_ffbc39f27901A1.aspx

Story Four

Four

Li Qingzhao: The First Female Poet for a Thousand Years

A portrait of Li Qingzhao

Chapter One

Happy Childhood

Our tale begins with the empire long divided. After the Tang dynasty (618-907 AD) collapsed, China suffered from continuous warfare. Later, Zhao Kuangying united part of China (see above map) and established the Song dynasty (960-1279 AD). This was at roughly at the same time that the Christian crusades against Islamic expansion had started in Europe. Even though China's commerce and trade were booming, and the civilians were relatively prosperous, it was not to last. The main threats to the kingdom were from its neighbours, the kingdoms of Liao and Xixia. This situation continued for decades, until sometime later, the Jin Kingdom replaced Liao Kingdom, and became the next threat to the Southern Song dynasty (1127–1279 AD).

The court stressed cultural developments over military expansion, and sought peace with its neighbours. The emperor was willing to sign treaties with the foreign tribes, and to buy peace with the Song's riches of silver.

Li Qingzhao was born in the year 1084 AD during the Northern Song period (960-1127 AD). Her father was a student of the scholar Su Shi, a famous scholar and writer who lived at the beginning of the Song dynasty. He had great influence on the scholars who came after him.

Li Qingzhao's mother was the daughter of a well-to-do family. She had an older brother, Li Ming, a high-ranking official of the court, who often spoiled his little sister. Perhaps more importantly, he borrowed from the court all the books that Li Qingzhao needed to expand her knowledge. He encouraged Li Qingzhao to follow in the footsteps of the family, and to become well-educated.

Li Qingzhao, like our other heroines, grew up in a free and intellectual atmosphere, with the opportunity to meet famous and celebrated people almost daily. Greatly influenced by her open-minded parents, Li Qingzhao became well-read and intelligent.

With the borders of the kingdom placated through finance, times were good, and the arts flourished. The famous painting, *Riverside scene of Qing Ming Festival,* reflects a typical market scene. The good times provided ample breeding ground for scholars and artists alike to flourish and expand their talents.

After the expansive style of the Tang dynasty, scholars of the Song dynasty developed a new style of poetry that was sung with music. At the same time, Confucian ethics had become more and more dogmatic, tightly regulating the behaviour of the people. This was especially so for one branch of Confucius' doctrine, Cheng-Zhu, which prevailed over all other moral doctrines during the dynasty. Family values were the core doctrine of the Cheng-Zhu school of thought. As for Qingzhao, at seventeen years old, and a little rebellious, she paid little attention to the dull doctrines of Cheng-Zhu. Especially as it ordered that women were not allowed to read or write, as society considered women without education or talent as virtuous. Women were to put the duties of the family first, and before marriage, girls were seldom allowed out of the home.

However, Qingzhao was lucky. She was encouraged to discuss politics and share her opinions with her father. Some of her opinions were advanced and full of confidence for a teenager, and a girl at that. Li Qingzhao was not only interested in reading the formal history books, but also unofficial history books and folk tales.

One day, she read an amusing story in a book from the Tang dynasty. It read: *The host sent out invitations to dinner to his guests. He also invited a famous singer to sing during the banquet. On a whim, the host decided he wanted to have some fun. He asked the singer to dress poorly, as if he were a servant. When the singer entered the room, nobody seemed to notice him, and when they interacted with him, it was with the air of superiority the upper class often used when addressing member of the lower class. He sat in the back of the room, silently, acting the part. Finally, the host mounted the stage, and said with a note of humour, "I would like to introduce one of my friends to you. He will sing a song to celebrate our time together."*

Everyone was silent, waiting in anticipation, looking around to see who the fellow was.

To everyone's astonishment, the poorly dressed 'servant' advanced.

The singer, now on the stage and fully composed, surveyed the audience and began to sing. The audience heard the clear and magnetic voice that lingered in the room. At first they giggled, as they realised the joke. Soon, though, they fell into silence as they were deeply touched by the sentimentality of the song. When the song ended, everyone remained silent, meditating and intoxicated by the narrative. Then, slowly at first, then faster, the applause grew louder and louder. They knew that the man dressed as a servant was in fact the best male singer in the Tang dynasty, Wang Baoshan.

Qingzhao burst out laughing when she finished reading the story. She found it amusing, but also thought how hypocritical the world could be, where people were judged as if they were the cover of a book.

Inspired by the famous scholars she read about, Qingzhao longed to write poems herself. Although there were already many poems circulating in society, most, to her mind, were badly written, especially, those that were written by men. The style of the poetry was too lavish and constrained. It was either about war or their personal ambitions. Li Qingzhao wondered if she could write poems and perhaps create a new genre of poetry. She felt poems should be refreshing and simple. She did not like using extravagant words to convey what she saw.

She wanted to discuss this with her father, who at that moment was in conversation with Wang Anshi, a famous scholar and a prime minister of the Song dynasty. She barged into the room and interrupted their conversation. Their discussion was about the dark clouds that rolled across the dynasty because of the threat of foreign tribes who cast greedy eyes on the wealth of the dynasty.

"Father, I want to write."

Her father, Li Gefei, smiled contentedly. However, Wang Anshi was astonished to hear Qingzhao's ambition. Though he was an erudite person, he was morally conservative. Wang Anshi was an obedient follower of the Cheng-Zhu school of thought. His son suffered from a mental disorder, so the father had him marry a girl from a poor family. The girl devoted herself to the care of her sick husband.

"Oh, Qingzhao you want to write?" Wang Anshi asked Qingzhao in surprise. There was a slight hint of disapproval in his tone.

"I write when I want." Qingzhao answered Wang Anshi's question straightforwardly, boldly staring at him with bright, intelligent eyes.

"I understand, after all you were born into such a family." Wang Anshi looked at Qingzhao's father and burst out laughing. He was embarrassed. Qingzhao sensed the irony in his tone and frowned deeply.

"Have you heard the story of Chen Yi's mother?"

"Yes, I have."

"Good, but nonetheless I will retell this well-known story to you. Have you heard of Chen Yi, the founder of Cheng-Zhu School? His philosophy is still followed by us today. His mother had devoted herself to her son's education. Chen Yi once wrote in his memorial that his mother was well educated before her marriage. *She had read all the history books. His grandfather was proud of his daughter's intelligence. Sometimes, he even consulted with her on political policy. His mother always gave wise comments, and when she did, his grandfather would sigh in pity, "What a fate! If only you were a boy." After Chen Yi's mother married, she hung a scroll on the wall with these words written upon, "Cheer up, my child! Devote yourself to your studies, remind your children to be diligent in their study." Imagine that even a woman like her dare not write.*"

"I am not alone! There are many women who want to be educated. I have made up my mind to write poems! I am starting now."

Wang Anshi burst out in derisive laughter. He took her words as nothing but a girlish wish.

Qingzhao, feeling greatly wronged, hurried out of the room.

Qingzhao loved the outdoors. As the youngest child of the family, she was spoiled by her parents, and was free to roam as long as she did not venture far. She was also free to make friends with whomever she liked.

It was early summer. She loved to see the flowers after the summer storms. The hills, covered in flowers, looked smoky from the distance. Qingzhao adored the sweet fragrance in the air. She lingered on the winding path for a long time, wishing she could stay for hours. When she was younger, she enjoyed going to the riverside to play hide and seek among the Lotus flowers with her friends.

One day, when her father went to the court, she took a bottle of wine from the kitchen and snuck out. She often had a cup of wine with her parents and assumed it would be okay if she was caught. She went to the West Pavilion, which was nearby, to meet with her friend Zhao Mingcheng, who she had known for several years.

After a while, the tall, handsome young man arrived. Qingzhao smiled and offered him a cup of wine. He drank it quickly.

After much giggling, they discussed poetry.

"Who is your favourite poet in the Song dynasty?" Qingzhao asked him.

Mingcheng thought for a while and said, "Of course, it should be Su Shi, your father's teacher. His style is grand."

"And, what do think of Su Shi's sister Su Xiaoxiao?" Li Qingzhao asked eagerly.

"She is talented. It is not surprising that she was able to gain a good education in that family. She must be greatly influenced by her bother."

While lying down on a bench, Qingzhao said in a languid voice, "I want to be like her, or even better than her."

"Ha-ha." Mingcheng offered her a challenge. "There are many famous and talented ladies in history. I expect you to be as good as they were."

"Do you?" Qingzhao's eyes flushed with excitement.

Mingcheng was born to the family of a current prime minister. He was tall for his age, with beautifully thick dark hair. He seldom laughed, and took everything seriously. He was devoted to reading historical books and writing poetry. However, he had a fascination with stones. He took one he'd collected from the riverside earlier out from his pocket. He showed it to Qingzhao, "What do you think of its shape?"

Qingzhao looked at it carefully and said without interest, "It's just a stone."

"Use your imagination. What does it look like?"

Qingzhao held the stone in her hands and observed, "Like a pearl?"

"Yes, that's it. That's the amazing thing about stones. Art originated from nature. Stones have different shapes and styles. My parents love collecting stones and gems from past dynasties because of their beautiful colours and shapes. We should try and understand the creativity behind stones."

"But it's still just a stone?" Qingzhao said with a dry laugh. Then she realised that she was being rude. She immediately shut up.

Mingcheng was annoyed with this shallow comment. He quickly returned the stone to his pocket and said grudgingly, "Women are always so short-sighted. You know nothing about art and beauty. There is more to stones than you think. If you observed the stone carefully you will find Chan philosophy embodied in them. When you take a stone or a gem in your hand, you will be amazed at the craft of nature. Much of history was carved in stone. The passing of time has weathered stones into different shapes."

Qingzhao nodded her head, pretending to be interested. Her eyes were half smiling, half mocking. In order not to annoy her friend, she laughed and changed the topic by saying, "Let's take a boat out on the river! The lotus flowers are out".

Mingcheng was happy to do this, though he was not as excited as Qingzhao. They found a boat by the side of the lake and took it out. The flowers bloomed in magnificent colours — white, pink, red and yellow — looking like an elegant, magic carpet covering the green lake.

Wine induced laughter echoed along the river, the laughter of nightingales. Mingcheng rowed the boat, while Qingzhao let her hand trail in the water. Seeing Mingcheng gaze at her stupidly, she splashed water into his face. He saw naughtiness in her eyes.

"There! There! Let's hide in the lotus flowers." Qingzhao urged Mingcheng eagerly.

He rowed the boat deep into a channel of lotus flowers. He stopped rowing and pulled in the oars, allowing the boat to drift at its whim.

Sitting in the low boat, the flowers towered over them. Qingzhao buried her face inside a big Lotus flower and giggled. They lay in the boat, looking up at the narrow band of sky in silence. The atmosphere was alluring, and they were intoxicated by nature.

Time passed fast, and the sun lowered in the sky. Qingzhao said, "Unfortunately it's time to go." Mingcheng sat up and started to row the boat back to the West Pavilion. However, after drinking so much wine, and in the dim light, they entered a wrong channel. "Are we lost?" Qingzhao asked.

"No, I can find our way." Mingcheng said blushing. Qingzhao ignored Mingcheng's answer, and said, "I think it is over that way."

Finally, they found the West Pavilion. As they stepped out of the boat, she saw the sun setting far away behind the mountainside. Qingzhao took in the scenery, and a poem from the Tang dynasty occurred to her:

> Lotus flowers dance on the river.
>
> The sunlight bathes the land red.

"It is Yang Wangli's poem," Mingcheng said with interest.

"I will write my own poems." Qingzhao mused.

Still annoyed at being lost, provocatively he said, "I don't believe it. Women can't write anything." He said while pulling the boat out of the water.

Qingzhao paid no attention to him, instead taking in the dusk and beautiful setting sun.

"What's the matter?" Mingcheng asked.

She smiled and said quietly, "Let's go. It's late. And you got us lost." Li Qingzhao burst out laughing.

Mingcheng knew that Qingzhao was teasing him, but his face was as red as a lobster.

习 习 习 习 习

Upon arriving home she bumped into her father unexpectedly. Her father stopped her and pretended to be angry, "Did you steal my wine? And why are your clothes wet?"

"I just went out to have a little fun… In fact, I wrote a poem about this afternoon."

"Oh, I would like to read it." He looked at her with a smile.

I'll always remember

in a boat on the West Pavilion.

Beautiful sunset,

Happily drunk, lost in the channels.

Where to go? Where to go?

The sea mews splashing the water, still…

She showed it to her father. Her father read the poem carefully, and found something special in it. It was quite different from the contemporary poetry. It offered a new format with its graceful and restrained style. In just a few lines she had managed to paint a full picture of a happy afternoon. The West Pavilion, the sunset, and even the sea mews, were all sketched distinctively. Simple as the poem was, it gave a fresh perspective. Moreover, the poem fully expressed a girl's enchantment with nature.

Qingzhao observed her father's reaction nervously and waited for his comments. Her father chuckled and praised her.

"Well done. I would like this to be published. Do you want to publish it in your own name?"

"Of course!" The girl said with elation.

"Good! You write better than your brother." The satisfied father said.

Qingzhao was a delighted that her father said that. She had high ambitions to write much better than her brother, so her poems would be accepted by the general public.

习 习 习 习 习

Printing techniques had been invented long before in the Song dynasty, and greatly helped the spread of literature. When Li Qing-zhao's first poem was printed, she immediately gained attention. It became a topic among both the high-ranking officials and common civilians. It was even quoted by the girls in brothels.

As a potential poet, Qingzhao had a woman's unique tenderness and keen instinct.

"Was it really written by your daughter?" many scholars asked Qingzhao's father.

"Of course," her father said proudly.

"Father, what is the public's reaction towards my poem?" Qingzhao asked her father eagerly after it was published.

"They feel it's a well written poem for a girl of your age." His father said encouragingly.

Qingzhao was not satisfied, pursed her lips, and rushed out of the room. She went to the garden and sat on the swing. She was dissatisfied. However, the beautiful scene in the garden soon mollified her. How sweet the smells were! She swung as high as the swing would go. The world seemed brighter. She closed her eyes and pondered how wonderful it would be if time stopped at this moment. Her mind turned to the *Book of Songs,* and she sighed, how romantic the love between men and women in the—

"My lady," she was interrupted by a servant, "how carefree you are! Please slow down. You are swinging too high." The servant urged. "We have been looking for you. A guest has arrived."

Qingzhao reluctantly obeyed her servant and got off the swing, asking casually. "Who is the guest?"

"The Prime Minister, Zhao Mingcheng's father."

Qingzhao blushed and hurried back into her room to write down her feelings.

I played on the swing,

when I was told a guest arrived,

Zhao Mingcheng's father.

No time to clean my hands,

sweat still on my forehead,

I hurried, without shoes on my feet,

the golden pin from my hair dropping on the ground,

I hurried with shyness.

Suddenly, I changed my mind, and looked back.

Only the sweet scent of green plum sprayed

on my face.

She put aside the paper and closed her eyes. It was so strange that she could not dispel the image of Zhao Mingcheng from her mind. She peered at the guest through the crack in the door, and pondered why Mingcheng's father had come.

She met the guest shyly and blushed. Zhao Mingcheng's father looked her up and down, as he conversed to her father about general matters.

칠 칠 칠 칠 칠

After meeting Zhao Mingcheng's father, Qingzhao threw herself onto the bed, confused, yet sentimental. She secretly had a crush on Mingcheng, but she could not speak openly to her parents about her attachment towards him. The beauty of nature only made her more sentimental and full of self-pity. She thought she was going to die from such sadness. However, she did not know these were just the sorrows of a young lady's secret crush and unrequited love. In emotional turmoil, she fell asleep. In a dream, she walked in thick fog, unable to find her way around. She finally saw a way out of the fog, and walked in that direction, only to come to a place full of hungry people. The road was covered with white bones. In horror, she turned back and ran, when suddenly a young man appeared in her dream. He looked very much like Mingcheng, but it was not him. She reached out her hands, trying to clutch his sleeves, but crowds of people swarmed and separated them. Qingzhao shouted loudly, "Please, please save me!" Suddenly, she woke up. It was just a nightmare. She poured herself a cup of wine. She had no idea at that time how prophetic that dream would be.

With these girlish sorrows, Qingzhao opened the door to look outside. The ground was wet after heavy rain. Flowers that were fresh and upstanding yesterday now lay silently withered and damaged on the ground. The ground was covered with a red blanket. Everywhere showed of the fury of the storm, with flowers withered, and the yellow willow branches still swinging in the declining wind.

Li Qingzhao was upset by the damage. She thought of the dream, which added to her sorrows. With these girlish sorrows in her mind, she picked up her bamboo brush and wrote:

Last night, the storm raged,

the wind violent.

This morning

the cool air could not make me sober

from my heavy drinking of last night.

I asked my servant, who rolled the shutter,

is all the garden so sad a picture?

"The Chinese flower crab apple is still blooming," she said.

Who knows? Who knows?

The leaves should have been green;

The flower petals should have been red.

Again she showed her father this last poem. He was secretly proud of his daughter's gift, and without telling her, ordered her latest two poems to be printed. His colleagues praised the talented young lady, who was just seventeen years old. These two poems expressed the sorrows of an unmarried young woman, who was sensitive towards nature and love. Even Wang Anshi changed his opinion after reading the poems and said to Qingzhao's father, "Li Qingzhao had created a new style of poetry. Few scholars in the current dynasty are able to write such clean and fresh prose. It's really hard to believe that such poems were written by a young girl."

The public started to acknowledge Qingzhao's talent, irrespective of her sex or age. In fact, the Song dynasty was a society full of contradictions. Even though the code of ethics ruled it was not proper that women be educated, a woman of rare talent was always highly valued and respected by men. Since Qingzhao became well-known, many writer and scholars visited her to discuss literature, philosophy, and sometimes politics. Qingzhao was greatly flattered, and received her guests warmly.

"Do you like the doctrine of Zhu Xi? Are you a follower of Confucianism?"

Qingzhao frowned and said, "I have read all his books. Yes, he was a great scholar of the Confucian school. He has made Confucius a God. There is great wisdom in Confucianism, such as the talks about ritual, music, education, knowledge and family values. However, Zhu Xi's school has made Confucianism too dogmatic. It is too limiting I am afraid... under the influence of Zhu Xi's school of Confucianism, society will be held back."

"Shouldn't history develop like this?" Another writer asked.

"I don't know, but if it continues developing in this way, I believe it will do more harm than good. Few people dare to speak out and say what they truly think. Life would be especially hard for women." Qingzhao, was animated, her eyes full of challenge.

"Why do you say that? Isn't Zhu Xi's school of Confucianism just one branch of Confucianism?"

"The most stupid thing about the Confucian school is that it lowers the status of woman!" She said with force.

"So, in your opinion, what kind of philosophy should we adopt?"

Qingzhao considered carefully, "I don't mean that I dislike the Confucian way complete. He was an erudite scholar, but I liked the expansion of the Spring and Autumn period (771-476 BC), and the Warring States periods (770-221 BC), when philosophical thought flourished. People thought with wider perspective, didn't they?" Qingzhao waved her hands and impatiently, indicating that she did not want to continue this topic as it upset her.

One scholar passed on Qingzhao's bold opinion to her father, who was immediately alarmed. He was shocked that his daughter dared to challenge the current ethical codes, and make such bold pronouncements. If he allowed Qingzhao to develop in this way, it may bring disaster to the family. He wondered whether he had spoiled his girl too much. He thought of all the possible consequences if the emperor heard what she said and broke into a cold sweat. It was time for Qingzhao to get married.

He discussed the topic of Qingzhao's marriage with his wife that night. After the decision was made, they turned their attention as to who she should marry. They found a good candidate as their son-in-law.

The next morning, Qingzhao was woken up early by her maid, who whispered in her ear. "My lady, do you know the master is going to have you married?"

"What?" Qingzhao immediately sat up in bed, "How do you know?"

"When I passed by the master and lady's door yesterday, I heard the master mention your name. I stopped and listened… Sorry, my lady, I don't mean to become an eavesdropper. But as it concerned you, out of curiosity, I listened."

"Yes, I understand. Did you hear whom they were planning to marrying me to?"

"I don't know. I vaguely heard someone whose family name was Zang."

"You mean that piggy, lazy, bossy young master from that big pretentious family?"

"Maybe."

"Oh my God!" Qingzhao rushed out and barged into her parents' room, who were still merrily discussing the potential marriage.

"Father, Mother, are you planning to have me married?"

"Yes." Her father said with authority, and a smile.

"To whom?" Qingzhao never saw her father so serious. She was a little surprised and scared at the same time.

"Who do you want to marry?" He asked her kindly.

Qingzhao sighed deeply, "I heard you would marry me to that no good for nothing, piggy and stupid playboy of the Zang family?"

"Zang?" It was her father's turn to be surprised, and burst out laughing.

"Who said I would marry you to the Zang's family?" The father looked at his daughter in amusement. The corner of his mouth rising.

"Who then?" Qingzhao was nervous, but at the same time, she was excited at the prospect of marriage.

"Zhao Mingcheng. We are to ask for an audience with the prime minister."

"Oh!" Qingzhao blushed deeply and ran out of the door squealing.

Her father let out an amused chuckle. He was planning a happy marriage between the two young people.

Chapter Two

The marriage

Qingzhao thought Mingcheng was just the right man – despite the fact that he was obsessed with stones. He had a striking appearance, much more outstanding than his peers. As for Mingcheng, of course he loved Qingzhao. He first realised his affection towards her when he was sixteen years old, and Qingzhao fourteen years old. They went outside and roamed the streets together during the Lantern Festival. Qingzhao was talkative and witty even then. She told funny jokes, and kept laughing all the time. Mingcheng was delighted. It was from that moment that he took Qingzhao as his wife in his heart. It was at this time when Mingcheng's father had brought up the topic of marriage. Mingcheng suffered sleepless nights, anxious and afraid that his father would have him marry someone else. Anxiously, he wished that his father knew who was in his heart. So he told his father, ambiguously, "Father, I had a strange dream last night."

"What was it?"

"I dreamed that I would marry a female poet."

His father was delighted. The only female poet at the time was Li Qingzhao, the daughter of the Li family. The father considered lady Li highly born, a good match for the family. Content, he went to the Li family home and confirmed the marriage for his son's sake. Qingzhao's father was ecstatic. The young couple married. The wedding, as one would expect of two well-to-do families, was large and full of pomp.

辛 辛 辛 辛 辛

Not long after their marriage, Qingzhao showed her husband a poem she had written before they married. It read:

> *I played on the swing,*
> *when I was told a guest arrived,*
> *Zhao Mingcheng's father.*
> *No time to clean my hands,*
> *sweat still on my forehead,*
> *I hurried, without shoes on my feet,*
> *the golden pin from my hair dropping on the ground,*
> *I hurried with shyness.*
> *Suddenly, I changed my mind, and looked back.*
> *Only the sweet scent of green plum sprayed on my face.*

Mingcheng burst out laughing. He realised his soul mate had fallen in love with him long ago, just as he had with her. He teased her, saying that their love was predestined. Qingzhao blushed and laughed too.

In the beginning of the marriage, both were happy. They did not have to worry about living expenses like other couples did. They spent most of their time composing poetry, writing couplets, and playing chess. He continued collecting stones and gems, but had grown to like antique jewellery and other small pieces as well.

Qingzhao loved plum flowers in the winter, and often arranged flowers on the table before she started to write poetry. She would burn incense to make the room full of heady scents. Then, in this cosy atmosphere, she would write.

"What news do you bring today?" she asked when Zhao Mingcheng came back from the court. She asked her husband about the antiques that he was collecting. "When did you start being interested in stones, gems and antiques?"

He replied, "I remembered that you once said stones were boring."

"Don't tease me. That was long ago." Qingzhao had a slight smile and continued, "Yes, it's true, but now that you taught me more about them, I have come to admire them". She tried to decipher the meaning of the ancient antiques, and enjoyed collecting them with her husband.

He explained to Qingzhao, "The study of gems and antiques can be traced back to the Shang dynasty, almost a thousand years ago. Look at this bronze ware. It's a medium-sized pot. On the surface it's carved with the characters 'The Emperor of Five Kingdoms'. History left marks on these objects, making them more valuable. But it is the secrets of history that we are discovering!"

"It is interesting. But in my opinion, beauty lies in being simple, elegant and soft, just like water. It is the same with traditional Chinese sketches, where an artist purposely left empty space, leaving people to think and wonder."

"That's it. You get it. Look at this." As he reached for a jade wine cup in the shape of a lotus flower. She carefully observed the cup – a real treasure. "How elegant!" she said with wonder. The cup shone under the ray of sunlight, crystal-like. "I have never seen such a beautiful wine cup. Usually, we use silver, but this cup is made of jade."

"The wine will taste better because of the jade. Ha-ha. It's pure white Hetian jade, with a narrow belly, and wider top. Look, it's translucent under the light."

Qingzhao played her hands over it, and could not put it down. This beauty inspired her. She loved learning the history of the pieces. She felt this inspiration helped her develop her poetry and unique style.

Qingzhao was at ease with her husband as they had a lot in common. Sometimes, when they went to bed, they ended up talking until dawn lit the sky. She insisted her husband tell her a story.

"My story today is about a beautiful stone in the east mountain-side. One day, the sky was shaking because two gods fought for power and punched a hole in the sky. The Queen Mother decided to use the stone on the east mountain to fill the hole. The stone, though, was arrogant, and showed no respect for the Queen Mother. The Queen Mother, annoyed by the arrogance of the stone, banished it to a desolate land far away. After many years, the stone was miserable for her mistake, but it was too late to apologise to the Queen Mother. While the stone languished in waste, another God felt pity for the stone and decided to convert it into the form of a perfect woman. Now..." he paused for effect, "this very woman is lying beside me...

I will always love you and never have a need for a concubine as many men do."

Qingzhao chuckled, and made love to Mingcheng with extra tenderness.

Sadly, the happiness of the marriage did not last. Ten years had passed and there was no child to bless the marriage. They began to quarrel over daily necessities. Yet, her love for him never diminished.

Moreover, Mingcheng felt the pressure of having such a brilliant wife. People knew him as Li Qingzhao's husband, rather than re-membering him for who he was.

It was at this time that Mingcheng was appointed as magistrate of a prefecture in Nanjing city in the southern part of China. This was far from the capital, and the appointment was to last for about a year. Hearing this news, Qingzhao was disturbed.

After he had departed, loneliness overwhelmed her. At night she tossed and turned in bed, and felt empty. She no longer had enthusiasm for poetry, or taking care of the antiques. When she woke up her pillows were wet with perspiration. She became moody and one day smashed her bamboo brushes on the floor, leaving the servant to clean up the mess.

However, though Mingcheng did indeed miss his wife and his comfortable home in the beginning, such feelings did not last long. After all, Qingzhao was no longer a young eighteen year old girl. Now, she was slightly over thirty. She had lost her youthfulness. The truth was he was bored with his wife. Though he was a man of strong will, he wanted to have a woman to warm his bed. Moreover, they were still childless. Mingcheng blamed Qingzhao.

One day, when Mingcheng strolled through the marketplace, he heard someone playing a Guqin nearby. As the music stirred his heart he followed the sound and discovered it came from a brothel. He hesitated a moment before entering, wanting to find out who was playing such evocative music.

When inside, he asked the madam, "Who is playing the music?"

The madam said it was in the new girl. She was born into a local, prosperous family, but the family's business had declined and finally gone bankrupt. Her brother had sold her to the brothel.

Mingcheng went upstairs and found the girl. She seemed shocked when the gentleman entered. She nodded her head shyly and took a deep bow. "My name is Xiang Lian."

"Oh, Xiang Lian. What a sweet name… What touching music!"

Xiang Lian judged the man in front of her timidly, but with a shrewd eye. She saw a handsome man, with a gentlemanly demeanour. Seeing this gentleman reminded her of her lost life. She could not help the tears that emerged.

Mingcheng, at first lost for words, asked, "Would you play music for me?"

Xiang Lian nodded her head, and played with tears on her cheeks. She could not stop crying when she sang about her life.

Mingcheng was enthralled, watching her sing and cry at the same time.

"Xiang Lian, why did your family go bankrupt?"

"My father had wronged a powerful official in the capital, whose name was Mr Li Gefei."

Mingcheng was astonished. It was the name of his father-in-law, Li Qingzhao's father. Suddenly, he felt sympathetic to this homeless girl. At the same time, rage swept over him. *How unfair to allow a girl who was barely eighteen years old be sold.* Qingzhao was charming, but she was a spoiled princess. He felt pity and protective over this girl in front of him. He sat and closed his eyes, listening to her music. He had made his decision. He would marry the girl and get her out of this lowly place. "Xiang Lian, I will take you out of here. Will you be my concubine?"

Xiang Lian bowed and shyly said, "Yes". There was no better destiny for a fallen woman than to marry into a good family, though she did not know Zhao Mingcheng was the son of a prime minister.

The madam offered a beaming smile. "Yes, Mr Zhao, you really have made a good choice. The girl is like a pearl in a crown... Now let's talk of her price..."

When the deal was done, Mingcheng smiled to himself. However, a troubled thought occurred to him. How would he explain Xiang Lian to his wife?

During Mingcheng's absence, for almost a year, Qingzhao kept sending letters to him almost daily. In the beginning she received warm responses, but soon he was too lazy to reply. *Men were too quick to change their mind,* Qingzhao thought with a sigh. She was depressed and worried, counting the days until his return. She had a thousand doubts in her mind. Sometimes, she took out a painting or other treasure that they had collected, and studied them, as if she could see her husband in the object. Her memories of their past were vivid. She remembered the bliss of their early marriage. But now he seemed heartless and paid no attention to her messages. At first he was just physically distant, now there seems emotional distance. Qingzhao's heart was aching.

One day, Wang Anshi came to visit her, "Ms Li, do you have any new poems to share with me?"

Qingzhao was glad to see him and put on a faint smile, "Sadly my inspiration has dried up."

"Then find it again. Never give up. I want to say that I was wrong before. You are really gifted. You have pioneered a different style of the poetry. The more I read your poems, the sweeter the taste lingers in my mind. Your poems are like orchards silently growing in a valley, attracting people with their fresh smell. I have to give up my pride, and acknowledge that women can write with ability."

Qingzhao smiled but said nothing as she raised her head proudly.

"Why, Qingzhao, you are depressed. Come out and have some fun? I will invite Zeng Gong (another scholar). We can drink wine and discuss history, literature and life."

Going out? How long had she jailed herself at home? Wang Anshi set a torch alight in her mind. Qingzhao summoned her courage, cheered up, and smiled, "Ok. Let's go boating and drinking."

习 习 习 习 习

Li Qingzhao, Zeng Gong, and Wang Anshi were on a boat, where they rowed into the lotus flowers, all the time laughing loudly. Qingzhao noticed, since autumn was coming to an end, most of the lotuses had started to wither – just like her beauty. She could not understand why Mingcheng had been silent for nearly a year.

"So, are you still thinking of your husband?" Wang Anshi laughed and asked, seeing Qingzhao sink into melancholy.

"No, never." Qingzhao said no as she did not want to lose face.

"Does he write to you?" Zeng Gong asked curiously. Qingzhao could see a trace of a smirk, as if he knew the answer. Her anger flared, realising her secret was exposed to the public.

"No." Qingzhao coughed to cover her embarrassment.

Wang Anshi joked. "Men, men! I bet he has another woman in his arms at this very moment. If a man really had you in his mind, he would find time to write to you. However brilliant your poems, you still can't escape your fate as a woman."

"I… I trust him." Qingzhao said with hesitation.

"Ha-ha, but you're doubting yourself." Wang Anshi said cynically.

Qingzhao felt chilled and shivered. In her confusion, and frustration, she quickly emptied her cup of wine. Then, she raised her empty cup to Wang Anshi, and said, "I have a poem."

Wang Anshi and Zeng Gong hurriedly took out paper and a brush, and with a challenging smile gave them to Li Qingzhao.

With the pink lotus flowers withering,
a chill creeps into my body.
I changed into warmer clothes,
and came out, boat rowing.
Seeing the clouds stretch in the sky
far away,
when is his letter to arrive?
When the wild goose returns home?
The moonlight shining fully on the pavilion.
The falling flower petals floating in
the river.

The river running dry.
Love sickness is enhanced by us two
living apart.
There is no cure for lovesickness.
The melancholy bites my heart
though a scowl had just passed away from my face.

"Brilliant." Wang Anshi said with delight. "It's a pity that men always fail to cherish such a blessing as you."

Qingzhao smiled modestly, "It still needs refining."

"It is touching." Zeng Gong said.

"Your poems are a thousand footsteps ahead of the rest." Zeng Gong commented.

"Thank you. I am just expressing how I feel and what I think, simply," she said generously.

"Well done, that's what makes a good poem."

Thereafter, there were waves and waves of laughter on the river.

彐 彐 彐 彐 彐

Many days later, Qingzhao finally received a letter from her husband. Hurrying, and with trembling hands, she tore it open, hoping for words of love. To her great disappointment, at first it spoke of prosaic things. The last few sentences gained her attention. They simply stated: *I have met a girl, Xiang Lian. I will marry her as my concubine.* He quickly described the girl's circumstances.

Stunned, she dropped the letter to the floor. She sat at her desk, her mind blank with shock. It was a pity that Mingcheng, who claimed her to be her soul mate, had no idea what love really was.

After calming down, Qingzhao replied in a challenging way. Her writing was full of irony: *We have only been apart for a short time, but already your mind has changed? Are you the same Mingcheng of my memory? The one who said he would never get a concubine? I don't recognise you anymore. I am strongly against you marrying another woman. I can't share my husband with another. It is blasphemy against our sacred marriage. You not only let me down, but also make both Xiang Lian and me miserable. I suggest you give her money and marry her off into a good family. Of course, I also have a lot of sympathy for her as a woman, but it will never be suitable for you to have a concubine. Please reconsider."*

Mingcheng ripped her reply into pieces. With clenched teeth, "What a tiger! It is normal for men to have a concubine. Why won't she agree to my union with Xiang Lian, and mock me instead? With what right does she humiliate me and challenge my right as a man? Just because she is a famous poet."

The more Qingzhao protested against the concubine, the greater Mingcheng's anger became. He had lost face. Mingcheng took up with Xiang Lian and ignored Qingzhao's letters.

Wallowing in her sorrow and anger, Qingzhao could only express the bitterness in her mind through poems. She waited anxiously waiting for her husband's return, and was greatly frustrated by the lack of response to her letter. Qingzhao leaned against the doorframe and watched the colour of summer fade away, as the autumn crept in with the first golden leaf falling. She was enmeshed in her sorrows. The sky looked bleak. She had no appetite, and became thin and haggard.

The Double Ninth Festival had arrived, and she began to lament:

Smoky cloud covered the sky,
worries grow unceasingly, never stopping.
The Double Ninth Festival arrived, again.
The jade pillow, and thin white curtain still.

The cold wind chilled me awake at midnight.
I drank a cup of wine in the east fence under the
sunset,
An aroma of yellow chrysanthemums,
lingers on my sleeves.
It's a lie to say that I was not depressed,
The west wind is blowing the curtain, waiting there,
growing thinner than yellow flowers.

Mingcheng's official capacity in Nanjing was unsuccessful. In fact, Mingcheng returned in disgrace. In the year 1129, there was discontent within his troops. His subordinates reported an imminent rebellion, which he did not take seriously. During the day he worked, but at night he played with Xiang Lian. His subordinates disobeyed Mingcheng's orders, and made preparation themselves to prevent the rebellion. When the rebellion happened, subordinate officers defeated the rebels. When the rebellion was suppressed, his subordinates looked for Mingcheng, only to find that he was with Xiang Lian, and was not even in the city. Mingcheng was summoned back to the capital because of his neglect.

It did not take long before Qingzhao heard the news of her husband's behaviour. She blushed, and could not help feeling shame. Finally, her husband arrived home, with Xiang Lian in tow. Qingzhao offered no smile of welcome, and felt a chilling coldness towards them both, but she could say nothing. Qingzhao was not the kind of scheming woman who hid her anger behind a smile. Normally, her frustrations found themselves expressed in her poems. Seeing this young and pretty girl, clutching her husband's arm, Qingzhao felt her head buzz. It was hard to recover her equilibrium. After they entered the house, Qingzhao went to her own room, and shut herself in.

Alone, Qingzhao felt numb. What will be will be. She would have to face this, sooner or later. She realised that her influence over her husband had diminished, and decided in that moment that her husband would not be her whole life. She would spend more time writing, to express her anger as well as her hopes. With these thoughts she felt a little better.

Mingcheng gently knocked on the door, and entered without being invited in. He found Qingzhao sitting with a frown. He put his hands on Qingzhao's shoulder and said, "Forgive me. I had no other choice. We have been married for more than ten years, and still you are childless. I love you, always and swear I only have you in my heart."

Qingzhao tried hard to squeeze out a smile but could not. She was confused, with an ache in her heart. She made little effort to talk, "I don't care. I'm too busy to worry about you." What she really wanted to say was, *Tear off your hypocritical mask, and get out!* However, she restrained herself and said lightly, "I have written many poems during your absence. But I finished a sad one only the other day."

"Can I have a look?"

Qingzhao showed two of her poems to him. As he read, he was immediately impressed by the deep sorrow that was expressed in them. At the same time, jealousy crept into his mind. He wanted to write better himself.

"How beautiful your poems are! Sorry for not responding to your letters. I thought of you day and night. If we corresponded with each other I would have been distracted from office."

Li Qingzhao simply said, "Never mind." As she thought *what a glibly-mouthed liar he is.*

"Can I borrow this poem?" he asked eagerly. He was always longing to outsmart his wife, for her famous name belittled him.

"Yes. If you want," was all she said, carelessly. She secretly longed for her husband to feel her sorrows by reading her poems.

Mingcheng took Qingzhao's poem, and shut himself into his own room for three days. He racked his brains to write a few poems. When he finished, he showed his poems, and his wife's scholar scholastic friend, Lu Defu.

"What do you think of these poems?" Mingcheng asked eagerly.

Lu Defu read each in turn, shaking his head all the time, until he stopped to read one a second time "The last poem is excellent. The others are not much good."

"Which is the good one?" Mingcheng asked eagerly.

"This one." It was Qingzhao's poem. Mingcheng felt greatly disappointed.

"Oh. Which sentence impresses you most?" Mingcheng said with disappointment.

"It's touching." He said simply, "Especially the last few sentences."

"Which last few sentences?" Mingcheng was eager.

Lu Defu smiled and read,

The cold wind chilled me awake at midnight.
I drank a cup of wine in the east fence under the sunset,
An aroma of yellow chrysanthemums,
lingers on my sleeves.
It's a lie to say that I was not depressed,
the west wind is blowing the curtain, waiting there,
growing thinner than yellow flowers.

"Oh!" was all Mingcheng could say, as a thousand emotions swarmed his mind. He knew he had broken Qingzhao's heart, but kidded himself that he had no choice, that they all were just victims of society.

刁 刁 刁 刁 刁

Besides the sudden appearance of Xiang Lian, the marriage between Qingzhao and Mingcheng was greatly affected by political conflict. The reforms that Wang Anshi had implemented had not succeeded, and so he was exiled to the southern part of China. All the parties involved were demoted from office. Qingzhao's father, being Wang Anshi's friend and associate, was implicated.

One day, when she was concerned about the demise of the fortune of her family, more news reached her, this time about her father-in-law. Soon thereafter, she stormed into Mingcheng's room and dropped a letter into his lap. Qingzhao said with spirit, "Look and see what your father is doing! He is eliminating his enemies in the guise of them not being loyal to the emperor. What a father-in-law! I don't know how the emperor turns a deaf ear and blind eye to what he is doing!"

"What are you talking about?"

Qingzhao said worriedly and with scorn, "The emperor is demoting all the party officials who are loyal to Wang Anshi because his reforms failed. I believe that Wang Anshi's reforms would do more good than harm."

"Yes, perhaps. But what does that have to do with my father?"

"He's eliminating any officials who have a different opinion to his. If Wang Anshi's reform is abandoned halfway through implementation, I cannot imagine the consequences." Qingzhao covered her face with her palm.

"What will the consequences be?"

"We will become slaves in a conquered country." Qingzhao said with a deep sigh. "According to the *Book of Changes*, if the reform is not fully implemented, there will be a disaster. As we all know, the emperor is a muddle-headed fool who is totally being led by your father!"

"Maybe it is not because of my father, but because Wang Anshi was too radical and arrogant to make friends with his colleagues in the court. That's why he was pushed aside by his enemies. As emperor, if half of the court spoke ill of Wang Anshi and against his reform, he would have no other choice but to drive him out of the court. Politics are just like a game of chess. Sometimes, for the sake of winning, the emperor has to sacrifice an important official who is loyal to him."

"Do you mean Wang Anshi is just a pawn in the game? The emperor is wrong to sacrifice Wang Anshi, with whose help he could have possibly won the war against the Jin Kingdom. We would have been stronger if the emperor had pushed forward with the reform! But he just condemned his loyal official so easily, as if he were insignificant!"

Qingzhao's face turned crimson from anger, "I don't want to argue with you on this. I have written a letter to your father. After you read it, you are free to give it to your father or not!"

With these words, Qingzhao left the room, leaving Mingcheng feeling inadequate. His common sense told him that his wife's words were right. Why did his father cause this disturbance? Did he really care about the Song dynasty? Or was he a traitor who received bribes from other kingdoms? When this horrible idea occurred to him, Mingcheng broke into a cold sweat. His dilemma was great, and he had no idea what he should do next. He wanted to ignore his wife's letter as if nothing had happened. However, he could not help feeling tortured by his own shame. He agreed that Qingzhao was right about Wang Anshi's reform. Finally, with determination, he sent the letter to his father.

∄ ∄ ∄ ∄ ∄

Mingcheng's father stared at the letter on his table. What was it about? This letter was written by his daughter-in-law, but sent by his son. He opened the letter and started to read,

> "*Dear father-in-law,*
>
> *As your daughter, I know it is improper for me to comment to you on political affairs, especially as a woman. But as far as my father is implicated, I have to comment.*
>
> *We all know that since the first emperor founded the Song dynasty, our country has grown stronger and prospered. The previous emperors loved literature, but saw little value in military leaders. In the beginning of the Song dynasty, the founding military officials were deprived of their military leadership. Luckily, heaven favoured our Song dynasty, and for many generations we lived in peace and harmony. However, according to the laws of nature, with the passage of time, our bureaucrats have rotted our system. Why not cut off the corrupted deadwood for the healthy growth of a big tree? As you are aware, we are facing a tiger, the Jin kingdom, and, in the southwest, a leopard, Xixia kingdom. We are surrounded by enemies! We need to strengthen our army, and at the same time, improve the living standards of civilian life by increasing the wealth of our nation.*
>
> *I know that Wang Anshi's reform was bold in many aspects, even bolder than Shang Yang's reform in the Qin dynasty. My dear father, you could take the best parts of the reform and bypass the weaker part. But,*

instead, you used it as a tool to eliminate people who
had different opinions to yours. I believe you should
push forward the reform for the benefit of the people,
and the people will adore and respect you. History
will remember you forever.
Do you have the courage to fight our enemies?"

Her father-in-law was so furious at this obviously impetuously written letter, he tore it up. *How dare a witless woman criticise my behaviour!* He quickly wrote a letter and called his servant.

"Master!"

"Take this letter and tell that seed of sin of a son of mine that from hence forth, all his family privileges are terminated. He will receive no wealth from me, and he is also to be deprived of his official position. Let's see how he is going to live with his beautiful scholarly wife!"

The letter stupefied both Mingcheng and Qingzhao. But when he was removed from his position at the court, the realisation came to him with a bang. He immediately sank into deep anguish. Why was his father so merciless and unreasonable, playing this move on him, his only son, just for the sake of a letter?

Soon, servants arrived at Mingcheng's home and drove him out of the comfortable residence. They also took most of his treasures. Qingzhao hurried to pack up her favourite books, while Mingcheng tried to save as many of his treasures and antiques as possible.

They were forced into cheap accommodation.

Without position, they became poor. This was too much for the privileged family, who were used to living in luxury. Mingcheng, Xiang Lian and Qingzhao moved constantly in order to live cheaper. The constant war between the Song dynasty and tribes in the north forced them towards the south, settling in Qingzhou city.

A storm may arise from a distant and clear sky, and the unexpected may happen. A few months after they arrived in Qingzhou city, Mingcheng had another shock – his father was dying from a sudden illness. Even on his death bed, he still did not forgive his son. Mingcheng was in deep anguish. The invading army from the Jin Kingdom covered vast areas of the Song dynasty territory, and swept through almost every city, trampling all in their path. Thousands were killed, towns were set on fire, and old palaces turned into ash.

Mingcheng and Qingzhao later heard that another prime minister, Cai Jing, had been appointed. Cai Jing was a cruel and conniving man, whose sole interests were power and money. Later, it became known that Cai Jing secretly colluded with foreign kingdoms accepting their bribes in exchange for betraying the secrets of the Song dynasty. In the court, Cai Jing persecuted members of the previous prime minister's clique, and Mingcheng, being the son of a former prime minister, was implicated. xThis brought even worse consequences for Mingcheng's health and his family.

Qingzhao started to like Qingzhou city, which she considered as an earthy paradise, far from political conniving. However, Mingcheng hated the idea of being a commoner. Soon, Mingcheng's health declined after the endless worry over his father, the poverty, and the constant fleeing from warfare took its toll. He had to stay at home, being taken care of by Qingzhao and Xiang Lian. Qingzhao virtually ignored Xiang Lian and always assumed control. She could never recover from the fact that Mingcheng found himself a concubine, and felt the girl had manipulated her husband.

During their escape towards the south, the family passed by the Wu River, the place where Xiang Yu, a King of Chu, had fought for the throne, before committing suicide after being defeated by Liu Bang, the King of Han. It was after he had lost face that he became unwilling to cross the river Wu to return home. Xiang Yu's tragic death had honoured him as a hero. Qingzhao looked at the flowing water on that rainy day and could not help being deeply touched. She wrote a poem *The Wu River*. Here is a stanza:

To be alive, is the hero.

To be dead, is the hero of ghosts.

This poem was heard by Mingcheng, who blushed out of guilt. He thought of his short official career and was ashamed of himself. He went into the room, lay on the bed and bemoaned his misfortunes.

Soon, another war started between the Jin Kingdom and the Song dynasty. It was the fiercest and bloodiest war the two kingdoms had fought. The Song dynasty had suffered a severe defeat. In the year 1126 AD, the troops of Jin Kingdom overwhelmed the capital city of Northern Song dynasty, Kaifeng. The two emperors, father and son, and other royalty were captured. Zhao Gou, the brother of the emperor, took over as emperor of the Southern Song dynasty. He ruled from Jinan city in the southern part of China. This marked the end of Northern Song dynasty.

Once again, Qingzhao's family were forced to escape, and followed the route to Jiankang city. Jiankang city was unbearably cold in the early spring. The white snow-covered walled buildings with black roofs stood bleakly by the riverside. The rain never stopped, and the trees looked gloomy adding to the dismal and cold look of the place. The broken walls and shattered buildings of the battlefield filled the town. Hungry people and stray dogs roamed without hope. Qingzhao saw it all. She was conscious that hers and everyone else's lives were broken. Not only had the love between her and her husband had ended, now their poverty was worse. Falling from the altar, princess to beggar, she almost had nothing of value, except a few antique treasures that they hoarded.

They moved into a shabby house, with war-broken walls and holes in the roof. What was worse, Mingcheng's health declined further. Without any willpower and dissatisfied with his life, it was clear he was dying. The unceasing rain exacerbated his bad temper and he refused to talk to either Qingzhao or Xiang Lian.

Qingzhao finally kicked open the door of Mingcheng's room, and entered to feed him a bowl of porridge. She tried to cheer him up, "Have this food. I cooked especially for you. Though I am not a good cook, I have tried my best. Please eat!"

"What day is it?" Mingcheng asked as he lay on the bed.

"It's the beginning of March. That's why it keeps raining. If you were to stand up and go outside, you would see a totally different world. The willow trees have just spurred new leaves that shimmer in the breeze, and look a deep green under the drizzling rain. The south is a vastly different picture from the north. Here, time has turned out to be slower and more pleasurable."

Mingcheng waved his hands tiredly, indicating he had no appetite, "I feel as dismal as the weather."

The smile disappeared from Qingzhao's lips. She was worried. It was pitiful watching this grown man lie in bed, with an angry scowl on his face. She could no longer bear such gloom and left to get some fresh air.

She wondered, *when will the rain and the wind stop? When will this nightmare end? Will the past and pleasant days ever return?* Qingzhao held out her hands, allowing rain drops to fall on her palm. Suddenly she burst out sobbing. The rain soaked her from head to foot. She seemed oblivious to it. What a stupid and self-important woman she had been in the past! Was there any justice in the world? How could she expect an evil and corrupt official to show kindness towards anyone? Those people, high in power, were like serpents, who would bite you as soon as look at you.

ㅋ ㅋ ㅋ ㅋ ㅋ

Mingcheng's health declined even further. To try and cheer her husband up, Qingzhao showed him the gems and stone antiques that she had carefully kept from being confiscated and avoided selling, despite their poverty. These were the only comfort for this miserable couple. "Remember this vessel? It was from Zhou dynasty. Sometimes, I wondered whether history moves forward or draws backwards. Whether the end of one history will be the beginning of another."

Mingcheng smiled weakly, "History is long. We are as tiny as a grain of sand and will leave no mark on history, forgotten."

She sighed and blamed herself, "How stupid and naive I am! I shouldn't have written that letter!"

Mingcheng, sensing the end of his life was near, softened and said, "We can't change what is past or our destiny. What is to come will come in its time."

Qingzhao smiled tiredly. "I wanted to thank you for teaching me about antiques."

"Thank you!" Mingcheng squeezed a weak smile. "Thank you for your company. You have been my soul mate since the first time that I encountered you. The war is cruel. The Jin Kingdom will soon trample this city. I'm sorry I can't accompany you to the end of your life…" Then changing the subject he advised, "You must follow the refugees along the emperor's escape route." Qingzhao understood that, so far, the emperor seemed resigned to retain sovereignty over a lesser part of the Song dynasty.

Qingzhao felt desperately tired. There was a lump in her throat, and tears on her cheeks.

"Promise me… you'll marry again."

"Don't say that."

He continued weakly, "You must challenge the norms of society and remarry." With clenched teeth and failing strength, he managed, "Let the whole world see how you, a woman can be famous! Ha-ha-ha." He stopped to coughed and then continued, "Please forgive Xiang Lian... and forgive me. Sometimes, I wonder whether my death is punishment for not being faithful to you. As to Xiang Lian, give her money, and let her go."

Qingzhao said nothing and lay her head on her husband's stomach, humming a song for him.

In a lighter mood, Mingcheng gradually closed his eyes.

Chapter Three

Second marriage

Not long after Mingcheng's death, in the year 1129 AD, the war between the Jin Kingdom and Southern Song dynasty had stopped temporarily. The brave but brutal Jin tribe were victorious and relentless. The common citizens suffered badly. Many were homeless and became refugees. Such a bloody war had caused the death of thousands of people.

Li Ming, Qingzhao's brother, and his family had also escaped the war. Qingzhao was taken in by Ming. Not long after her husband's death, Qingzhao's father died of consumption as he had exhausted himself on the endless journey. This was another shock to Qingzhao, who had a great affection for her father.

The long road was dust-laden from the fleeing traffic. Qingzhao's face was grim and dirty, and aged virtually overnight. The more they escaped to the south, the more heartbroken she became. Living on the road as they did was hard, and the rain and wind took a toll on her health. She took out her handkerchief and sneezed. The handkerchief was blackened from the dust in her nose. Probably, she would never return. She hated to acknowledge the fact that she was now part of the conquered people of the Jin Kingdom.

They settled in Wenzhou, a city in the deep southern part of China. At the same time, the capital of the Southern Song dynasty had moved to Hangzhou city. Her brother supported the family financially. Qingzhao, like other refugees, did not complain about their miserable life. She took all that life gave to her, including misfortune and sorrow.

Many scholars, including Qingzhao, expected that the new emperor Zhao Gou to rally the forces and drive out the troops of the Jin Kingdom. In the beginning, Zhao Gou swore that he would fight and win back the lost territory. However, the rich life in the south quickly reduced his ambition – his citizens were forgotten.

Qingzhao worried about the failing Kingdom endlessly, and the plight of the people and their suffering. She expressed her anger in her poems for all to read. She missed her precious life and her previous home in the north, when the dynasty was strong, and when her married life was in harmony. One time, Qingzhao held on to the gate, and looked through the rain towards the north whilst sighing.

A poem formed in her mind:

Who plants the plantain trees under my window?
It's wet in the middle of the room.
Wet in the middle of the room.
Each leaf, with the jumping heart, wet.
The clouds stretching, horizon to horizon.
Nothing expresses my sorrows.
I lie awake,
in the middle of the night,
it's still raining, heavily.
My pillows wet with tears.

Rain drops, one after another.
Tear drops, one after another,
play on my mind.
I listen to the rain,
falling on the plantain leaves.

Qingzhao's poems were still welcomed by the entertainment girls in the south, even though these girls could hardly understand what she meant because the dialect was different. Qingzhao wished her voice could be heard by the emperor, and that he would act.

习 习 习 习 习

Upon waking up one morning in 1133 AD, she heard the good news that Han Xiaoxu had been summoned by the emperor to visit the two captured former emperors of the Northern Song dynasty, Zhao Huan and his father. Hearing this news, Qingzhao was hopeful; there a glimpse of light in the darkness.

Han Xiaoxu and Qingzhao had been friends for years. Their friendship had been fostered by their grandfathers. She cheered up and wrote to Han Xiaoxu in support.

For me, whose grandfather was a friend of your grandfather, I have to say that unfortunately our family business declined in recent years. I feel I have no face to continue our friendship.

I heard that you are to visit Jin Kingdom to negotiate for the two captured emperors. This is good news. God is still here! As a writer, I dare not speak too much. So I made up a poem, offering you support.

In May of third Shao Xing year, the Gaozong emperor had been on the throne for a long time.

Your duty is the mission

though the times are difficult.

Remember not to boast of your achievement.

Foolish fidelity and piety is unnecessary.

Please alight the coach and start your journey.

To capture the foreign tribe with a whip in your hands.

No diplomat more fit to take the mission

than you, most capable one.

No one should forget that your grandfather

served the previous emperors for many years

as high as a prime minister,

liked by the common people.

The emperor of the Han dynasty had a majestic air.

Even the Hun tribe removed their caps to show respect.

In the Tang dynasty there is a famous General Zi Yiling,

who was as brave in war,

making Hun Kingdom pay tribute to the Tang

without losing a single solider.

The majesty of Han dynasty is not declining.

The foreign tribes are frightened.

When you climbed the white jade stairs in the palace

representing the Emperor

you are not a common man!

Our generation has come to the south for a few years.

We have already become refugees, without a homeland.

I only have to give you my best wishes for success.

Han Xiaoxu received Qingzhao's letter and was deeply touched. He delighted in the fact that she was so patriotic and attached to her homeland. Even if she was low and depressed, her patriotism was still strong.

With these sentiments, Han Xiaoxu's envoy started the journey to the north. He was uneasy, for he was afraid that he may fall into a trap set by the cunning and strong Jin Kingdom. He was worried that negotiations would fail, and he would not be able to bring the two former emperors back. What was worse, he was afraid that King of Jin would have him poisoned at the banquet that would surely be held upon his arrival. With a thousand entangled feelings, Han Xiaoxu reached the Jin Kingdom. The very land that they stood on had once belonged to the Song dynasty.

Upon arriving, dusty and tired, he informed the messenger of his name. A few moments later, a smiling, muscular man emerged. He was abrupt in manner. However, he carried a generous air. Han Xiaoxu guessed the man must be the King of the Jin Kingdom.

"Ah, my dear ambassador from the Song dynasty, welcome to our territory!"

"Ha-ha. Time has changed so fast. In the vicissitudes of life, the world has turned upside down, and black has turned to white, but the land is still ours." Han Xiaoxu laughed.

"Ha-ha, who can claim in law that the territory that we now possess should belong to the Song dynasty forever? We warriors fight for our territory. The victor is king, and the loser becomes a thief. You would be a fool if you believed a wolf would give back the meat that was already in his mouth."

Han Xiaoxu smiled and said with dignity, "I did not come here to quarrel. According to our agreement, you allow me to visit the two emperors to confirm their well-being."

"Of course. But let us not hurry. Come, have tea and food. Refresh yourself."

Once inside, Han Xiaoxu sat down and boldly ate the food as if he had not a care in the world, showing no signs of fear in case the food was poisoned.

The King of Jin said with a pretence of surprise, "So, your emperor in the south still has concerns for his brother?"

"Of course. He is a generous and open minded emperor who is deeply attached to the citizens of his dynasty."

With a sneer, the king scoffed, "Interesting… But is he willing to pay a reasonable ransom for his brother and father?"

"Yes he is, as he is a filial emperor. But first, I need to see if the two emperors are in good health."

The King of Jin signalled to an aid and a few moments later two escorts marched the two emperors into the chamber.

"Han Xiaoxu!" they exclaimed in surprise.

Han Xiaoxu instantly saw their diminished health and confidence – it was obvious that conditions were harsh. They struggled to free themselves from the escorts, but in vain. When they saw Han Xiaoxu standing there, their dim eyesight suddenly brightened. The two broken men gained a glimmer of hope. Instantly, they stood taller, squared their shoulders and gained a more majestic air. Even so, their hearts beat furiously. They doubted they would ever be released.

Before they could communicate, the King of Jin made another gesture to the escorts to take the men away. The two emperors immediately folded in alarm. Panic filled their faces as they begged, "Han Xiaoxu, please save us!" These were the last words of these two shameful emperors, who had abandoned their kingdom whilst indulging in worldly entertainments. The plight of the two captured emperors made Han Xiaoxu's flesh creep. He blushed and felt a little ashamed. His imposing manner had been weakened relatively.

Han Xiaoxu could see that his mission was going to be a difficult one. He felt he was merely a pawn of the higher echelons on their chessboard.

"I must take the two emperors back with me." Han Xiaoxu cleared his voice and recovered himself finally.

"Ha-ha. Yes, but with two conditions…" he held up a finger, "firstly, your emperor must acknowledge that the territories that we occupied will forever belong to us."

Putting up his second finger, "You will pay tribute of ten thousand silver pounds a year for three years."

"Impossible."

"If your emperor refuses to pay the ransom, your whole dynasty will be trampled by our soldiers' feet. And the life of the two emperors will also come to an end. They will become ghosts."

"It's our territory." Han Xiaoxu countered, "You are a thief."

"We are not ashamed of taking it from you as the spoils of war. History always stands on the winner's side."

Han Xiaoxu restrained his anger, "Your demands are too arduous."

"Your emperor in the south is rich. These are our conditions. Agree to them and we will return your two emperors to the Southern Song dynasty." The King of Jin grinned happily, showing his white teeth.

"Is this the final deal, no other conditions, no hidden agenda?"

As if surprised, "No, of course not. You can trust me!"

Han Xiaoxu rose from his seat angrily and said to the king, "I will convey your terms to the Emperor. But know that your arrogance will stand against you in the future!"

"Ha-ha-ha." The King of Jin laughed it off. "We will wait and see who the heavens favour."

Han Xiaoxu ignored his words and angrily left the palace, climbed into his coach and led the envoy back home. The haste he made left dust in the air long after they had departed.

The moment Han Xiaoxu was back in the Southern Song, he went to report to the emperor. However, when Han Xiaoxu entered, the emperor did not notice him, as he was enjoying the pleasurable company of two women who lay on the floor at his feet. With a discreet cough, the aide gained the attention of the emperor. Han Xiaoxu had to wait for the giggling to stop.

"What news?" The Emperor did not even raise his head.

"He will release the two emperors if you pay a tribute of ten thousand silver pounds a year for three years... and... he demands you acknowledge that the stolen territories will forever belong to them... Otherwise..."

"Otherwise what?"

"He will execute both of the captured prisoners and he will trample our land under his soldiers' feet, again."

"Damn!" The Emperor threw the pillow to the floor, which nearly hit one of the girls' heads. The Emperor waved his hands and said, "You can retreat now."

"How should I reply to the Jin Kingdom?" Han Xiaoxu asked, lowering his head.

"Do we need to give him a reply?" There flashed madness in the eyes of the Emperor.

Han Xiaoxu felt deep anguish and disgust. He wanted to say something, but restrained himself. He realised that at this moment the emperor was blind. He felt safe in the south corner of China, closing his eyes to the threat of the Jin Kingdom. He ignored the oath he had made to save his brother and father. The reason why he sent Han Xiaoxu was just to play political games. He wanted to show the common citizens that he himself was a sage and sincere emperor, who dared to risk everything for the sake of the kingdom and his captured relatives. Even if he could not save them, at least he made a show of it.

When back home, he thought of the letter that Li Qingzhao had sent him before his departure. Frustrated, he took this out and replied.

My dear friend Qingzhao,

You will always be my friend, no matter what has happened to your family name.

The world has changed so fast, quite beyond our imagination. The sea has turned into the field, and the field has changed into the sea, and the good old times can never return. Shamefully, I have to report that I have failed in my mission. The two emperors will probably not be returned, and we will be attacked, again!

Qingzhao read the letter with trembling hands. When she had finished, she looked at the drizzle in despair. She could see no future for the dynasty. She wiped tears from her eyes with the back of her hand. A poem, *The hope in the spring*, written in the Tang dynasty by Du Fu expressed her sadness:

The country is broken,

yet, the mountain and river remain the same.

The grass in the city is tall and wild.

The seasonal flowers still blossom brightly,

spilling tears of pollen,

the passing of the birds, so disturbing.

Misfortune after misfortune – it was too much for Qingzhao. She descended into a deep depression, and then ill health. Exhausted and weak, she had no desire to do anything. No interest in reading or writing. She lay on the bed, staring at the roof.

Ming summoned the doctor. The doctor felt her pulse, and prescribed her herbal medicine.

In order to cheer Qingzhao up, Ming insisted another man come into Qingzhao's life – Zhang Ruzhu. Ming thought maybe a lover would enliven his sister, and give her enough hope to live. Perhaps with a man she would not feel lonely or desolate.

Zhang Ruzhu was an acquaintance of Qingzhao's brother. He heard of the death of Qingzhao's husband from Ming, and came to stay. He often took care of Qingzhao and fed her the herbal medicine. He was kind and tried to pacify her sorrows. "You have much!" Zhang Ruzhu comforted her, "you can't abandon your life and your work."

Qingzhao finally revived her will, and slowly regained her appetite. She was grateful for Zhang Ruzhu's encouragement and support. Yet, she was still anguished that the country was broken!

Finally, summer arrived, and the rains departed. After staying in bed for four months, Qingzhao was weak but recovered. She went outside, allowing the sun to bathe her and melt the ice in her heart. Maybe, there was a hope. She was determined to be strong.

It was around this time that there was some gossip about the letter Qingzhao wrote to Han Xiaoxu prior to his mission to save the former emperors. Soon, enemies made false allegations against Qingzhao, saying "The Li family was secretly sending treasures of gems to the Jin Kingdom. The Li household is full of valuable antiques, which were of such value, they could buy the entire Kingdom."

The gossip came to Qingzhao's ears. It never rains but it pours. It not only brought shame to the family name, but also wronged the scholar's character.

The charges claimed that she and her brother illegally stored treasures from past dynasties. The enemies wanted the family broken. Qingzhao clenched her fist indignantly. She valued the integrity of her family name more than wealth and would not let treacherous people break her down. She wrote to the emperor with sincerity and persuasively, stating that her whole family is devoted to the Song dynasty, both before and now. In order to show her loyalty, she was willing to donate her few remaining items to the court, to prove her family's sincerity.

But it was at this time that the King of Jin acted on his promise to destroy the Song dynasty and marched southwards. Again, the government of the Song fled. Many lives were lost, and many cities left in ruins.

The government in the Southern Song headed further south to a remote area. Qingzhao and her family followed the same route, as refugees, running for their lives.

Zhang Ruzhu went with them, and supported Qingzhao along the road. During this chaotic time, she was grateful for his support. Ming, as head of the family, suggested that Qingzhao and Zhang Ruzhu marry as soon as they could be settled. Although she did not love him, this seemed to be pragmatic.

Chapter Four

Divorce and Jail

In the year 1132, when Qingzhao was about forty-eight years old, the Li family finally settled in a household in Hangzhou, the new capital of the Southern Song dynasty. The war was over for now. It was then that she and Zhang Ruzhu married.

It was well said that a long distance tests a horse's strength, and a long time can reveal a person's heart. After the marriage, Zhang Ruzhu finally showed his true nature. It transpired that he was a cold hearted man, who was extremely adept at emotional violence. On the wedding day, in order to crush Qingzhao's pride and exert his control over her, he refused to sleep with her, and slept in another room. Qingzhao felt scorned. Nevertheless, she told herself that she married not for love, but for safety.

The next morning, Zhang Ruzhu asked, "Qingzhao, what is the value of your treasure? Our treasure!"

She just shrugged.

He then pointed to a painting on the wall, "The value of this?"

"It's from Han dynasty, but unfortunately, the original was ruined in the war. When my first husband was alive, we made a copy of it, so this one is a fake."

His face turned red. He picked up a vase on the table, and dropped it to the stone floor, where it smashed to pieces. "Is this a fake as well?"

Qingzhao said in mockery, "That was not clever. That vase was valuable."

Zhong Ruzhu immediately regretted his impetuous action, and looked like guilty little boy.

"Oh. What kind of vase was it?" Zhang Ruzhu asked, trying to hide his guilt.

"It was from the Tang dynasty, a rare prunus vase." Qingzhao said with pretend nonchalance. The prunus vase is a small-mouthed, short-necked, thin-bottomed, round-based vase. It was named as such as only winter sweet flower branches can fit inside.

"Why didn't you tell me before?" Zhang Ruzhu roared.

"It never occurred to me that you would be so stupid as to break a beautiful vase." Qingzhao challenged, her eyes holding him in her gaze.

Zhang Ruzhu was so furious that he left the room and slammed the door as he went.

Qingzhao was also shaking with anger. She finally understood why Zhang Ruzhu wanted to marry her. It was not for love – he was after what he thought was her wealth. Qingzhao refused to be silent. She frowned, and made up her mind that she would fight him tooth and nail.

Zhang Ruzhu returned home in the evening drunk. "You bitch. How dare you lie to me? It's just a common vase, nothing special."

"But for scholars it is very valuable." Qingzhao smiled calmly.

Zhang Ruzhu was about to slap her face but pulled back at the last moment. He decided to use another tactic, "How dare you laugh at me. As your husband, I forbid you to read or write. If you dare to read a single word or write a single poem, I will burn all your papers."

And with that he left the house again, to amuse himself with the whores of the town.

Qingzhao was not so easily bullied. She carefully considered her options. Quickly, she searched for a place to hide her writings. She searched every nook and cranny of the house, until she noticed an obscure cabinet. Upon opening the door, and looking within, there was large blue package that she did not recognise. She locked the door for privacy and opened the package. Her heart jumped as precious jewellery flopped onto the table. *Where could this have come from?* She wondered. But then she saw a note. Curiously, she opened it and started to read. It seemed to be an account. Qingzhao's heart beat faster. Her quick instinct told her that this is important. It could be evidence to compromise Zhang Ruzhu.

She read:

> *The following is a record of funds received by myself, Zhang Ruzhu, whilst in the services of the Song Dynasty, as commander of No. 9 army troop in the defence against the Kingdom of Jin.*
>
> *Receipts from:*
> *The coordinator of the troops: 1,000 silver coins, plus rations and goods foraged after battle as commission for ignoring various actions by the coordinator.*
>
> *500 silver pieces from a junior officer who wanted a promotion.*
>
> *Receipt of the painting "The Goddess of Luo River" by* Gu Kaizhi, *in the year 400 AD from the Jin dynasty for information given.*
>
> *From the Jin, a gift of a beautiful vase which I sold for 1,000 silver pieces.*

Qingzhao kept reading down the page.

Qingzhao's hands were shaking. *How dare he make a fortune when the dynasty was in crisis? And now he wants what little I have.*

She stood up and paced the room and finally came up with an idea. She would expose her husband's crime to the emperor and ask to be given an Imperial divorce!

ㄱ ㄱ ㄱ ㄱ ㄱ

This was a risky move as in those times. There was a law that stated that if a wife exposed her husband's crime, if the husband was proven guilty, she and her husband would both be sentenced. Qingzhao hid the note against her bosom. The next day, she wrote a letter to the emperor and announced her husband's crime. She included the incriminating note. She wrote in the letter that she would hand over the jewellery when it was demanded.

The entire court was astounded that a woman's loyalty to the dynasty was so great that she risked jail or death by exposing her husband. With such undeniable evidence, the emperor's men went to the Li house and took Zhang Ruzhu away in chains, along with the evidence. The sentence was announced. Qingzhao was sentenced to three months jail. Zhang Ruzhu was sentenced to one year. Zhang Ruzhu cursed Qingzhao severely by spiting on the floor at her feet. The emperor granted Qingzhao's request of divorce and the unhappy one hundred days of marriage came to an end. She raised her head high as she was lead to jail.

During his one year in Jail, Zhang Ruzhu was bad tempered. When set free, he was deprived of all official titles and fell into poverty and shame. He never forgave Qingzhao.

While serving her sentence, Qingzhao was disgusted by the filth and cramped quarters. She survived by knowing she was innocent, and with the philosophical belief that it would end soon enough, and she would be without her horrid husband. She shared the damp cell with rats, fleas, and the ghosts of past occupants – as well as other prisoners who bemoaned their misfortune. She sank into deep agitation. Grime covered the one small window high above head height, so it let in minimal light. She longed to feel the sun on her cheeks, and breathe fresh air. The food, if it could be called that, was swallowed with revolt. She ate it in order to survive. She summoned her courage and held onto her faith and tried to remain positive. Although it was only three months, the ordeal seemed to last years.

The day of her freedom arrived, the jailer came with his big bunch of keys. He was surprised to see Qingzhao, the famous poet who had revealed her husband's crime, was able to bear the dark and terrible environment. The jailer marvelled at her courage as he opened the door of her cell, saying that she was free to leave. Qingzhao shuddered with relief and could not get out quick enough to the fresh air. The sunshine, seemingly brighter than she remembered, made her squint. Yet she peered around her. *Life was bittersweet*, she thought, knowing she would cherish life more after staying in the dark, inhumane jail.

However, bright as it was outside, her life was still in ruin. Her ever loyal brother had sent a servant to the jail to bring her to his home.

The news of Qingzhao's second marriage and divorce with Zhang Ruzhu had reached the public. There was much gossip, and many laughed at her. With her reputation in shreds, and no longer regarded as the goddess of poetry, admiration turned to scorn.

Wang Anshi wrote a letter to Qingzhao, blaming her for her troubles and for being imprudent.

My dear friend Li Qingzhao,
I have heard of your divorce from your second husband.
That is not a good thing. Worse, though, your exposing

your husband's guilt to the public was a terrible mistake. Women should obey their husbands, irrespective of the husband's behaviour! There are many virtuous women in history that chose to be buried alive with their husband when they died. They knew their duty. Because you have ruined your reputation, even with your brilliant writing, who is going to read your poems now? You must forgive me for being blunt, but I give you this advice as a sincere friend.

Wang Anshi.

Qingzhao gave an emotionless laugh, scrunched up the letter, and threw it in the fire.

One catastrophe followed another. With all the pressure and the lack of proper food in the damp jail, she descended into fever. She had a high temperature for three days, and became ghostly thin. She was not expected to live. Being taken care of by Ming and the doctor, she finally recovered.

However, her spirit was not broken, and she would not be broken by the opinions of the public. The moment she recovered from her illness, she used her bamboo brush to compose poems.

In this way, Qingzhao continued to live in her brother's residence. She was forty-eight.

Despite her brother's support and care, she never really felt that it was her home. There was tension between Qingzhao and her sister-in-law, who would have preferred not to have been associated with her. Qingzhao still retained a few treasures, which she passed on to her brother. She required only a small room in the corner of the courtyard, trying her best to not be a burden, where she fully devoted herself to reading and writing.

She composed new poems, full of the stories her bittersweet life and her current loneliness. The past floated in her mind, and was gone with the wind.

When these poems were published, just as in the past, they quickly spread far and wide. Many sighed with pity for the misfortune and decline of status of Qingzhao.

I seek, and seek,

feeling cold and small.

Everywhere desolate, depressed, shabby.

Spring is arriving,

the weather still cold.

Too cold to sleep

With a thousand entangled thoughts

I leave my bed,

drink wine.

How can I bear the heavy wind on such a night?

A goose passed by,

full of sadness.

It looks as if this scene happened long ago.

The yellow flower petals fall to the ground,

after a spring storm.

Thinner and older I am.

Who dares to pick up these flowers?

I wait by the window,

how can I bear to see?

The bright day turn into dark night?

Rain beat the Chinese parasol,

in the evening, one drop after another.

At this moment, how could I use one word

to describe my boundless sorrow?

彐彐彐彐彐

At this time, a young ambitious woman named Zhang Shuyu visited Qingzhao to study her writing and poetry. Since she was a child, she had been a great fan of Qingzhao. She wished to be another Qingzhao in ability.

Qingzhao was glad that this girl was her pupil. She was generous, and taught her all she had learned. And, as they became friends, Qingzhao shared her story. However, luck did not favour Zhang Shuyu, as her poems were rejected by the public as conservatism became more prominent.

When Zhang Shuyu tried to enrol in formal studies of the classics, she was mercilessly rejected by the school, because she was a woman!

Chapter Five

The later life of Li Qingzhao

Qingzhao, now in her fifties, was even more rebellious. Her poems had loftier sentiments. As an elder lady, she was no longer afraid of authority or society, who placed her in metaphorical chains.

She wrote with pride and arrogance:

The setting sun is glorious,
melted gold.
The clouds in the evening are bold, and colourful,
shining transparent jade.
Where are the people I seek in such beauty?
The newly grown leaves, tinted the trees, smoky.
The plum blossom falling on the ground
hints of sadness.
The smell of spring… scented with fragrance.
In such beautiful weather of the Lantern festival,
how could we know that storm and wind
will disappear suddenly?

Those friends, who rode luxurious carriages
invite me to join them.
Modestly, I decline.
I remember the glorious days in Bian Jin city,
of leisure in my girlhood chamber.
Especially, I enjoyed that Lantern festival.
We wore jewels, and jade in our hair,
and golden necklace around our neck,
Each girl carefully made up.
Now, I am old, tired.
I have no care to make up my hair.
I would rather hide behind the curtain, near the window,
to hear the laughter of other people passing by,
echoing in my ears.

Qingzhao felt old and spent a lot of time living in the past. After suffering so much, she finally found peace in her old age. She was at peace with her past of fame, marriage, betrayal, and love. She asked herself whether she had been wrong in her past actions.

习 习 习 习 习

Li Qingzhao died in 1151 AD. She was about sixty-seven years old. After her death, her poems still had a great influence on scholars in later centuries. She was honoured with the title 'The first female poet in a thousand years'. Her poems were collected by scholars. Many were lost, but the poems they recovered were placed in a volume.

Bibliography:

Li Qingzhao (1084 AD-1155 AD): Born in Jinan, Shandong province. She was born into a rich family and well-educated. During her first marriage with Zhao Mingcheng, the couple were devoted collectors of antiques. When the Jin Kingdom invaded the central plains of China, Li Qingzhao escaped to the southern part of China with the refugee government.

The style of her poems changed from reflecting a carefree happy life to showing deep concern towards the fate of the dynasty and her love sickness towards her husband. Her husband died not long after he married a concubine. During the escape from the Jin, Zhang Ruzhu was introduced into her life. Zhang Ruzhu married her for the treasure in Li Qingzhao's family. Li Qingzhao discovered Zhang Ruzhu's crimes and asked for a divorce with Zhang Ruzhu openly from the emperor. When Li Qingzhao recovered from her broken marriage, she devoted herself to writing. She had a peaceful old age.

Zhao Mingcheng (1181 AD-1029 AD): An official and scholar of the Song dynasty. In 1103 he married Li Qingzhao. His career as a statesman was not smooth. He was dismissed from his officialdom by his father because his wife wrote an offensive letter. He died in 1129, during the family's escape from the Jin.

Zhang Ruzhu: Born in Zhejiang province, he achieved first prize in the Imperial exam in the late Northern Song dynasty. In the first Shao Xing Year, he was appointed an official, and in the second Shao Xing Year, he married Li Qingzhao, not for love, but for the treasure of Li Qingzhao's family. His crimes were discovered by Li Qingzhao, who asked for a divorce in public. It was unclear how he lived in his later life.

Xiang Lian: Zhao Mingcheng's concubine, a fictitious person. Zhao did indeed have a concubine, but her name is unknown.

Wang Anshi (1021 AD-1086 AD): A famous thinker, politician and writer. In the year 1042, Wang Anshi won first prize in the Imperial exam and entered officialdom. He had achieved relatively good success. In 1069, he insisted on reforming the Northern Song dynasty, which was rejected. He was demoted from office. Depressed, Wang Anshi died in Zhong Mountain in the southern part of China.

Han Xiaoxu (1074 AD-1150 AD): Born in Henan province, he was the grandson of Han Zhongyan, a prime minister in the Northern Song dynasty. He was successful in his official career, and a friend of Li Qingzhao. He once acted as an ambassador to negotiate with King of Jin. Before he left, Li Qingzhao wrote him a letter of encouragement.

Books:

1. *Encyclopaedia of China,* November 1986, P392-P394
2. *A collection of words,* 1989, Shang Hai Ci Shu publishing House.
3. Li Xinzhuan, *The important history after Jian Yan year.*
4. Fan Chong, *The record of Shen Zhong period.*
5. *The history of Song dynasty, about Wang Anshi,* in the volume 227.
6. *The history of Song dynasty,* volume 379

Scholarly research:

Ronald Egan (艾明诺) The burden of being a talented woman: discussion of Li Qingzhao's character from her early thoughts. California

Ye Fang, *The discussion of Li Qingzhao's poem before and after she escaped to the south.* Zhe Jiang province.

Yao Xia, *Li Qingzhao's traveling and making friends,* Shan Dong province.

Huang Shengzhang, *Li Qingzhao's lifelong story*, the third volume in 1967, in Literature studies.

Internet sources:

Li Qingzhao's poems: http://www.shicicn.com/zuozhe/2908.html

www.ingramcontent.com/pod-product-compliance
Lightning Source LLC
Chambersburg PA
CBHW060031030426

42334CB00019B/2272